"PLACE ON THY H
OF THE PRECIOUS
AND FEAR NOT

"TRI

NOV
MAN

O

JESUS, MARY

by

FATHER S
Msgr. Austin P. B

Direc

The CONFRATERNITY of

at the Monastery

5300 FORT HAMILTON PARKWAY
BROOKLYN, N.Y. 11219

TRIPLE NOVENA MEDAL
of JESUS, MARY and JOSEPH

is carried by Confraternity Members in a League of Novena Prayer.

NOVENA means any nine consecutive days or nine consecutive Fridays of prayer for one's personal and Confraternity intentions (page 33).

MEDAL shows Jesus shedding His Blood on the Cross ... Mary at left: "Behold thy Mother" ... and at right, Joseph: "Go to Joseph." This medal daily reminds us to live in the presence of Jesus, Mary and Joseph, and to put all our trust in them.

"JESUS, MARY, JOSEPH"

Confraternity of the Precious Blood
Made in U.S.A.

Foreword

THIS NOVENA MANUAL has been arranged for Members of the Confraternity of the Precious Blood. Like the Novena Medal of Jesus, Mary and Joseph, it features devotion to the Precious Blood of Jesus ... to Mary Immaculate from whom Jesus drew the first drops of His Precious Blood ... to good St. Joseph, the guardian of Him who redeemed us by His Precious Blood.

On Dec. 8th, 1925, our Most Rev. Bishop, Thomas E. Molloy, S. T. D., imparted his public blessing to the Apostolate of our Confraternity, erected at the Monastery Chapel of the Cloistered Sisters Adorers of the Precious Blood. Since that time, the Monastery Chapel has become, for our members, a pilgrimage center of devotion to the Precious Blood of Jesus Christ.

The countless graces received during the Novenas, recall the words of Father Faber in his book "All for Jesus," written for the Confraternity of the Precious Blood: "It is this Blood which merits all good things for us. I assure you I have sometimes felt quite nervous as, week after week, we were called upon to read at the Friday meetings the numerous letters recording the wonderful and speedy answers which God hath vouchsafed to our prayers."

We are grateful to Mr. Arnott J. White for many art designs.

May Jesus, Mary and Joseph, by the merits of the Precious Blood, bless those who use this Novena Manual.

Imprimatur

✠ FRANCIS J. MUGAVERO, D.D.

Bishop of Brooklyn

August 5, 1975

Contents

O Jesus
when my sorrow
seems
too much for me
to bear
I'll come unto Thy
holy shrine
and lay my bur-
den there

Each Friday 🍇 during the
Novena to Jesus, Mary, Joseph

and the NOVENA MEDAL

THE CROSS symbolizes the Sacrifice of Jesus. It was the first altar on which Mass was offered. His Precious Blood flowed on it for our salvation. The Cross is the sum-total of Christian life: "Take up thy cross daily and follow Me."

The history of the Cross is a history of miracles gained by those who carried its symbol on their persons, and in their hearts by prayer and sacrifice. And so the Crucifix on the Novena Medal is most appropriate for every Catholic to carry. It is a constant reminder of devotion to Prayer, to the Sacraments, and to Holy Mass: all those living realities of religion purchased for us, as St. Peter says, "not with silver or gold, but with the Precious Blood." « *See page 28.* »

"He shed His Blood for me, to the very last Drop."

MARY

and the NOVENA MEDAL

MARY also suffered a crucifixion as she stood by the Cross, so close was her Immaculate Heart to His. "Two hung on one cross," according to St. Alphonsus. Hence, says saintly Pope Pius X, "Mary became Dispenser of all the gifts that Jesus purchased for us by His Precious Blood."

The MIRACULOUS MEDAL

OUR LADY'S OWN GIFT

Its design revealed to Bl. Catherine Labouré in Paris, 1830. Mary Immaculate promised graces in abundance to all who would wear it as a shield, putting themselves under her care. « See page 31.»

"Behold Thy Mother"

and the NOVENA MEDAL

IN all their needs on earth, Jesus and Mary went to Joseph. Pray him to watch over your family as he watched over Jesus and Mary.

Family Unhappiness? GO TO JOSEPH! The Holy Family was a happy family and Joseph was its guardian.

Unemployed? GO TO JOSEPH! He was a worker, a carpenter. Appeal to him. He understands.

Sickness? Afflictions? GO TO JOSEPH! His care enabled a mother in agony to bring the Comforter of the afflicted into the world with a roof over His Head.

Sorrow? GO TO JOSEPH! Life crucifies us at times. Turn to the sympathetic heart of Joseph. He is the guardian of the "crucified." « *See page 33.* »

"Go To Joseph"

JESUS MARY JOSEPH
BE WITH US ON OUR WAY
AS WE PRAY

God respects our prayers not for how elegant they are, but how SINCERE they are.

We should pray often and everywhere; yet the Church is the special place for prayer, because God is in the Church as He is in no other place on earth. He is there in the Sacrament of Mercy both as God and Man. Pray with **CONFIDENCE.** "Whatever you ask for in prayer, BELIEVING, you shall receive." « Matt. 21-22 » Nothing is more pleasing to our Lord than our TRUST in Him. "Can a woman forget her infant? ... and if she should forget, yet will I not forget thee." « Isaias 49-15 »

Pray with **CONTRITION.** A person in mortal

sin who refuses to give up his life of sin is an enemy of God. He can hardly expect God to heed his prayers. God promises however to receive the soul who repents. "Turn ye to Me ... and I will turn to you." « Zach. 1-3 »

Pray with **FERVOR   ATTENTION.** "Much love," says St. Augustine, "but not many words when thou prayest." "What do you say when you pray to Jesus?" St. Theresa was asked. "I don't say anything, I love Him."

Pray with **PERSEVERANCE.** If your prayers are not soon answered KEEP PRAYING; because, says St. Hilary: "The obtaining of grace depends mostly on PERSEVERANCE in our prayers." Let Jesus be our model ... "And falling into an agony He prayed the more earnestly." « Luke, 22-43 »

Pray with **RESIGNATION.** "Father, not My Will but Thine be done." God does not prescribe merely what will make our life sweet on earth, but only that which will save us from eternal death.

A Day in the Cloister

In spirit let us pass beyond the Grille which separates the Cloister from the outside world

Begin the day in the Chapel for Hour of Reparation.

Sleep, then rise for one hour's meditation before God's Mirror, the Crucified Jesus, that His Image may be engraved in the Sister's life. Followed by Mass at 6.30, uniting with Priest in offering the Precious Blood.

Breakfast, followed by Monastery duties.

Recitation of Divine Office in Chapel, followed by work until 11.45, keeping in mind their motto: "To adore, make reparation and suffer with fidelity, constancy and generosity."

Examination of Conscience—Spiritual reading during dinner (and at supper). Recreation from 12.45 to 1.30 P. M. "Rejoice in the Lord always." Prayers for deceased Benefactors.

Spiritual Reading (fifteen minutes). "What such and such a one has done for God, why cannot I do?" Then work in a spirit of reparation.

Stations of Cross at the hour Christ

died (for deceased benefactors and conversion of sinners), followed by Divine Office. Work until 5.30.

Rosary and Benediction. As spiritual mother, prays for us all to the Mother of us all. Then meditation until 6.30, sitting like Mary Magdalen at His Feet, listening to His Words.

Supper, etc., followed by Recreation and Mary's Litany for Missionaries.

Evening Prayers for Community and world, etc., before the Tabernacle. "Stay with me, Lord, the day is now far spent." Prayers for souls in Purgatory, followed by sleep.

Such is the day of a Sister Adorer of the Precious Blood —*one continuous act of adoration, thanksgiving, reparation, and petition*in union with Jesus, offering His Precious Blood throughout the world in the Holy Mass, "from the rising of the sun until the going down".

Our Sisters maintain perpetual adoration of the Most Precious Blood in the Cloistered Choir of their Chapel. The Blessed Sacrament is exposed on the First Sunday of each month. The Forty Hours' Devotion is held four times a year by special permission of the Pope.

Mother Catherine Aurelie
AND THE SISTERS ADORERS
OF THE PRECIOUS BLOOD

HOW DEVOTION to Jesus, Mary and Joseph brought our cloistered community of Sisters Adorers into being is told in the life of Mother Foundress Catherine Aurelie of the Precious Blood « born in St. Hyacinth, Canada, July 11, 1833 « died there July 6, 1905.

In a play at graduation young Aurelie as St. Catherine was inspired to devote her life to the Precious Blood. "I feel in me all the energy of the Divine Blood. It is a generous Blood which aspires only to be shed."

For eleven years she walked a sorrowful way, her spiritual directors unable to decide what religious community she should enter. "I thirst," the cry of Christ on Calvary, ever called within her heart. "I thirst" for souls. "I also thirst," repeated Aurelie. "I am ready to sacrifice

14

all, to show You how much I love You, and how much I desire to see You loved by others."

She was sent to leading theologians « finally to the Archbishop of Montreal. He advised: "Go into a small, secluded dwelling and establish a new cloistered community of adorers of the Precious Blood, daughters of Mary Immaculate."

Hesitation for two years by the new Bishop of St. Hyacinth; then on the Feast of St. Joseph he prayed as an indication of God's Will, that his doubts might be replaced by confidence. His petition was granted. In 1861 the decree went forth, establishing this new cloistered community. In 1896 it was finally approved by Pope Leo XIII as a world-wide Institute.

In thanksgiving to Jesus, Mary and Joseph, the first three sisters were called Mother Catherine Aurelie of the PRECIOUS BLOOD, Sister Elizabeth of the IMMACU-LATE CONCEPTION and Sister Euphrasia of ST. JOSEPH.

Mother Aurelie's faith and holiness grew unto marvels and miracles. "I would be as a magnet to attract all hearts to myself in order to give them all to Jesus Christ." Heroic young women were attracted to her work. Thirty-one Monasteries have since been established in Canada, United States, Italy, Cuba, China and Japan.

TRIPLE NOVENA PRAYERS

TO

Jesus, Mary, Joseph

« *Pages 17, 18, 19, 20, 21, 23, 29, 31, 33* »

Every Friday, at several services, thousands of local members unite with our Cloistered Sisters at the Monastery, reciting prayers on above pages.

*Two Sisters Kneeling at Cloister Grille
Before Altar*

Mass **Clock**

MASS
TRAVELS
WITH SUN

POWERFUL
PRAYER FOR
EVERY HOUR

¶ Central U.S. Time is listed as practical for entire U.S., since Holy Mass is offered during the three hours from 5 A.M. to 8 A.M.

¶ Locate on World–Mass–Clock that part of world where Mass is now being offered (at this hour); then unite your sacrifice with Christ's Sacrifice as you recite this prayer.

ETERNAL FATHER, through the Immaculate Heart of Mary,¹ I wish to unite myself with Jesus,¹ now offering His Precious Blood in (*mention name of country*) in the Holy Sacrifice of the Mass,¹ for the needs of Holy Church,¹ the conversion of sinners,¹ the relief of the souls in Purgatory¹ and for the special grace I here implore.
« *Mention request* »

WE SPEAK TO GOD

. . . in a Plea for Instruction . . . as outlined in Holy Mass from its beginning up to and including the Prayer.

PRIEST: In the Name of the Father, etc. | We will go unto Thine altar, O God. | From this holy mount send forth Thy light and Thy truth | so that we may learn as we pray.

PEOPLE: We confess to Thee, Almighty God, | that we have sinned exceedingly in thought, word and deed. | Therefore, we beseech the Blessed Mary, ever Virgin, and all the Saints | to pray to Thee for pardon and absolution of our sins.

PRIEST: Then in all things, may we | give glory to Thee on high | and receive Thy peace on earth | promised to men of good will.

PEOPLE: Incline Thine ear, O Lord, to our petitions | and bring light to the darkness of our minds, | that we may never lose sight of the suffering of our Savior | or of our share in His Resurrection. Amen.

GOD SPEAKS TO US

*. . . in revealing Divine Truth
from the Epistle to the Creed.*

PRIEST: O Holy Ghost, Spirit of
Truth, | we wish to show ourselves
thankful to Thee, | for instructing us
that Jesus is the Son of God, | and that
we are redeemed through His Blood.

PEOPLE: Lest we be choked by the
cares and riches and pleasures of life, |
do Thou recall to our minds that our
citizenship is in Heaven, | since at
Baptism we received adoption as children of the Father.

PRIEST: Grant, then, | that we may
be of one mind towards one another |
according to Jesus Christ | so as to
glorify the Father of us all.

PEOPLE: O Holy Spirit, | ours through
the grace of Confirmation, | may we
ever be witnesses for Christ, | even to
the very ends of the earth, | and under
Mary's care may we advance with
Him | in wisdom and grace before God
and men. Amen.

WE GIVE TO GOD

. . . in a Self-offering with Jesus from the Offertory to the end of the Eucharistic Prayer.

PRIEST: O Eternal Father, | we wish to unite our poor finite sacrifices of the coming week | with the infinitely pleasing Sacrifice of Jesus | suffered on Calvary and renewed in Holy Mass.

PEOPLE: May our offering of bread and wine on the altar | represent our personal gifts and sacrifices | and recall also how Jesus, as our High Priest, | offered Himself at the Last Supper.

PRIEST: May the mystical separation of the Body from the Blood of Jesus during the two consecrations | remind us of their actual separation on the cross, | when He was immolated as our suffering Victim | to atone for our sins and unite us with Thee.

PEOPLE: It is truly meet and just, therefore, | that we give Thee thanks, | because through Him and with Him and in Him | our offering of praise and reparation is made acceptable to Thee, | God the Father Almighty, | in the unity of the Holy Spirit, world without end. Amen.

GOD GIVES TO US

. . . the Bread of Life and Union in the final Act of the Divine Drama beginning with the Our Father.

PRIEST: Our Father, Who art in heaven, | we, Thy children, now make bold to say: | Give us this day a hunger for the daily Bread | by which we truly live in Thy peace and love, | free from the fascination of earthly things.

PEOPLE: May our reception of Jesus, | ever coming to us as a Glorified Victim, | and still bearing the five wounds in His Risen Body, | remind us that His Resurrection is the proof of Thy acceptance | of His redeeming Sacrifice | even as it is the pledge of our own resurrection.

PRIEST: We pray Thee that the more often we receive Jesus, | the more surely will He nourish our soul with spiritual food, | and protect our body with temporal aid, | so that we may ever hold fast to Thy commandments.

PEOPLE: May all of us who partake of the one Bread, | be of one mind and heart in Divine and fraternal charity, | until we are all united with Jesus | in the fulness of His Mystical Body | at Thy heavenly Banquet. Amen.

ACT of THANKSGIVING

ACCEPT, O most merciful God, the Sacrifice of Thy Son, in thanksgiving for all the benefits Thou hast granted me.

Thou hast created me to Thine Own Image and Likeness. Thou hast redeemed me with Thy Son's Precious Blood. Thou hast called me to the true faith, and preserved me from eternal death, which I so often deserved for my sins.

What return shall I make Thee for these and all Thy favors?

I offer Thee Thine Only Son, Who offered His Lifeblood on the Altar this morning, uniting my little sacrifices with His great Sacrifice; and thus I am able to make a real thanksgiving for all the blessings Thou hast bestowed on me and on all mankind.

¶ *"But where are the nine"* who did not return to give thanks? asked Jesus, of the lepers He healed by a miracle. We petition God for graces needed. Do we thank God for graces received? If not, we offend God by ingratitude.

Prayers for the Beatification of Mother Catherine Aurelie

O JESUS, Who didst inflame the soul of Thy servant, Catherine Aurelie, with an ardent zeal for the glory of Thy Precious Blood, grant, we beseech Thee, that the halo of "BLESSED" may soon be placed upon her brow, and that the favors we receive through her intercession, may show forth the power of Thy Adorable Blood, draw all souls to Its worship, and fill them with a spirit of love and reparation.

O MARY, Immaculate Virgin and Mother of the Word Made Flesh, intercede for us with Thy Divine Son, and obtain for us from Him, the favors we implore, through His humble servant, Catherine Aurelie. Amen.

¶ *Numerous graces have already been obtained through her intercession. You are asked to report any such favors.* « See page 14 »

SORROWFUL MOTHER NOVENA

In each of the following Stations, we behold Jesus through the eyes of Mary.

¶*Make one station each day at home during your Morning or Evening Prayers. Jesus revealed to a Saint: "However grievous the load of a man's sins, he may take comfort in the hope of pardon" by meditating on His Passion and Death.*

1. As a Novena, make the Way of the Cross for at least nine or more consecutive Fridays (each day our Cloistered Sisters make the Stations at 3 P.M.— the hour at which Jesus died).

2. Read and meditate on the following 14 Stations, pages 25, 26 and 27.

3. Say the Sorrowful Mother Novena Prayer (page 30). Pray for Confraternity intentions (page 33).

Pope Benedict XIV recommended the Way of the Cross as a source of SPIRITUAL BLESSINGS. St. Leonard, who erected the Way of the Cross in 652 places, emphasized it as the source of many TEMPORAL BLESSINGS.

LIVING WAY of the CROSS

¶ *Mary was the first one to make the Way of the Cross. She made it with Jesus Himself. In each of the following Stations, we behold Jesus through the eyes of Mary.*

Jesus Is Condemned To Die
"God Through Sin I Crucify" 1.
Repeat following after each verse

Jesus, Mary, Joseph, pray
Help me walk this "Living Way."
Mary, sorrowing, hears the death sentence: "Crucify Him! His Blood be on us." O! Mary, hear my prayer: "Blood of Jesus, be my redemption."

Jesus Bears The Bitter Cross
"Bear Me Up In Grief And Loss" 2.
Mary, uncomplaining, sees the Precious Blood flow from the wound in His Shoulder. O! Mary, help me to shoulder my cross patiently, in union with Jesus.

Jesus Falls In Blood And Woe
"Sins Of Mine Have Struck Him Low" 3.
Mary, sore distressed, sees the parched earth quickly drink up His Red Life. O! Mary, when my soul is parched by earthly desires, recall to me the words of Christ, "He who believes in Me shall never thirst."

Son And Mother Meet In Pain
"Must They Grieve For Me In Vain" 4.
Mary, brokenhearted, sees Jesus in agony. Jesus sees her in anguish. O! Mary, inspire me with contrition and penance for causing such sorrow.

25

5. Simon Helps To Bear The Load
"Lead Me Too Along Thy Road"

Mary, bewildered, sees all refusing to help Jesus. O! Mary, even as I ask Jesus to help me, may He ever find me ready in Catholic Action for home and foreign missions.

6. On A Cloth He Prints His Face
"In My Soul Thine Image Trace"

Mary, calm in grief, sees Veronica brave the fury of "the crowd." O Mary, by the grace of Confirmation, may I never fear what "the crowd" may say or think.

7. Struck To Earth Again By Me
"Help Me Rise To Follow Thee"

Mary, in pain untold, sees the Cross crush Jesus, yet He rises. O! Mary, obtain for me the strength to rise and follow Christ as my Leader.

8. Weep For Sin He Tells Them Here
"Jesus Make My Grief Sincere"

Mary, suffering, sees Jesus suffer from desertion by His own, yet even now He comforts others. O! Mary fill me with zeal for the Spiritual Works of Mercy.

9. Thrice He Falls By Lashes Torn
"In Thy Blood I Rise Reborn"

Mary, crushed in spirit, sees Jesus helpless, prostrate in the dust. O! Mary, lest I fall again, help me to prepare worthily and make proper thanksgiving at Confession and Communion.

26

Stripping Christ They Tear His Skin **10.**
"Help Me Tear My Flesh From Sin"

Mary, torn from Christ, sees Him torn from the robe she made for Him. O! Mary, strip me from all that stains my baptismal robe.

In His Hands They Drive The Nail **11.**
"In Thy Hands I Cannot Fail"

Mary, pierced anew, sees wells of His Redeeming Blood dug in His Hands and Feet. O! Mary, in His Wounds help me renew my Baptismal Vows and with those nails bind me to Jesus forever.

Jesus Dies His All To Give **12.**
"By Thy Death Teach Me To Live"

Mary, overwhelmed, sees Jesus die, His Bleeding Wounds pleading for me. O! Mary, place one drop of that Redeeming Blood on my sinful soul.

Mary As You Take Your Son **13.**
"Take Me Too When Life Is Done"

Mary, mourning, receives her dead Jesus from the altar of the Cross. O! Mary, help me to receive the living Christ from the altar of the Mass with something of your reverence and love.

Buried Christ Who Died For Me **14.**
"May I Rest At Last In Thee"

Mary, now desolate, buries in death the Son to whom she once gave birth. O! Mary, renew thy motherhood over me now and at the hour of my death. Amen.

HONORING HIS 7 BLOODSHEDDINGS:

*1—Circumcised. 2—Agony. 3—Scourged.
4—Thorn-crowned. 5—Carries Cross. 6—Crucified.
7—Heart pierced.*

LORD, Thou bearest me written in Thy Hands in letters of indelible red, which are Thy most Holy Wounds, and to inspire me with confidence Thou gently sayest: "I have written thee in My Hands with the marks of My most Holy Wounds."

Therefore, will I ever say to Thee: "Read, Lord Jesus, read that handwriting and save me through Thy Precious Blood."

O Sacred Heart of Jesus, I have asked You for many favors, but I plead for this one.

Take it, place it in Thine open, broken Heart, and when the Eternal Father sees it, covered with the mantle of Thy most Precious Blood, He will not refuse it, if, in His infinite and farseeing Wisdom, He sees it is best for my spiritual and temporal welfare. It is not alone my prayer, but Thine. « *See page 7.* »

APPEAL TO DIVINE PROMISES

O JESUS, Who hast said, "Ask, and it shall be given you; seek, and you shall find; knock, and it shall be opened to you," with Mary, Thy Most Holy Mother, and through the merits of Thy Most Precious Blood, I seek, I knock, and I ask that my prayers may be heard. *Glory be to the Father, etc.*

CIRCUMCISION

AGONY

O JESUS, Who hast said, All that you will ask the Father in My Name, He will give you, with Mary, Thy Most Holy Mother, and through the merits of Thy Most Precious Blood, I humbly and earnestly ask that my prayers may be heard. *Glory be to the Father.*

SCOURGING

CROWNING WITH THORNS

ETERNAL FATHER, I offer Thee the Most Precious Blood of Jesus Christ, the merits, love and sufferings of His Sacred Heart, the tears and sorrows of our Immaculate Mother, as the price of the favor I wish to obtain, if it is for Thy glory and my salvation. Amen.

CARRIES CROSS

CRUCIFIXION

HEART PIERCED

29

HONORING HER 7 SORROWS:

1—*Simeon's prophecy.* **2**—*Flight to Egypt.*
3—*Jesus lost.* **4**—*Way to Calvary.* **5**—*Jesus dies.*
6—*Descent from Cross.* **7**—*Jesus buried.*

HAIL, MARY, full of sorrows, the Crucified is with thee; tearful art thou amongst women, and tearful is the fruit of thy womb, Jesus. Holy Mary, Mother of the Crucified, give tears to us, crucifiers of thy Son, now and at the hour of our death. Amen.

O MARY, Mother of Sorrows, I beseech thee, by the bitter agony thou didst endure at the foot of the Cross, offer to the Eternal Father, in my name, thy Beloved Son, Jesus, all covered with Blood and Wounds, in satisfaction for my sins, for the needs of Holy Church, the conversion of sinners, the relief of the souls in Purgatory, and for the special grace I now implore. Amen. *Mention your request.*

MARY IMMACULATE NOVENA

O MARY IMMACULATE, Lily of Purity, I congratulate thee, because from the very first instant of thy Conception thou wast filled with grace. I thank and adore the Most Holy Trinity for having imparted to thee favors so sublime. O, Mary, full of grace, help me to share, even though just a little, in the fullness of grace so wonderfully bestowed on thee in thine Immaculate Conception. With lively confidence in thy never-failing intercession, we beseech thee to obtain for us the intentions of this Novena « *mention them* » and also that purity of mind, heart and body necessary to unite us with God. Amen.

SIMEON'S PROPHECY

FLIGHT TO EGYPT

JESUS LOST

WAY TO CALVARY

The MIRACULOUS MEDAL

M AY thy special aid be granted to those who wear thy Medal.... May it be their strength in combat and their all powerful shield against their enemies. ... May it bring consolation to those who weep, solace to the afflicted. ... May it, at the hour of death, be the pledge of a glorious eternity. . . . Amen. O Mary, conceived without sin, pray for us who have recourse to thee.

JESUS DIES

DESCENT FROM CROSS

JESUS BURIED

HONORING HIS 7 JOYS:

1—Told of Incarnation. 2—Angels adore Infant. 3—Gives Name to Jesus. 4—Adoration by wise men. 5—Prophecy of salvation. 6—Return to Nazareth. 7—Jesus found in temple.

O GLORIOUS St. Joseph, appointed by the Eternal Father as the guardian and protector of the life of Jesus Christ, the comfort and support of His Holy Mother, and the instrument in His great design for the Redemption of mankind; thou who hadst the happiness of living with Jesus and Mary, and of dying in their arms, be moved with the confidence we place in thee, and procure for us from the Almighty, the particular favors which we humbly ask through thine intercession. « *here ask the favors you wish to obtain* »

P RAY for us, then, O great Saint Joseph, and by thy love for Jesus and Mary, and by their love for thee, obtain for us the supreme happiness of living and dying in the love of Jesus and Mary. Amen.

APPEAL TO ST. JOSEPH

O BLESSED ST. JOSEPH, tenderhearted Father, faithful guardian of Jesus, chaste spouse of the Mother of God,
I pray and beseech thee to offer to God the Father, His Divine Son, bathed in Blood on the Cross for sinners, and through the thrice Holy Name of Jesus, obtain for us from the Eternal Father, the favor we implore... Amen. « *See pg. 9.* »

TOLD OF INCARNATION

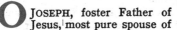
ANGELS ADORE INFANT

O JOSEPH, foster Father of Jesus, most pure spouse of the Virgin Mary,
pray for us daily to the Son of God, so that, armed with the might of His grace and loyally fighting the good fight here on earth, we may be crowned by Him at the hour of our death. Amen.

GIVES NAME TO JESUS

Confraternity Intentions. *After praying for your own needs, do not forget the dying plea of Jesus, "I thirst" for souls. 1. Conversion of a non-Catholic; 2. Return to faith of a fallen-away Catholic; 3. Relief of a soul in Purgatory. (Mention names.)*

ADORATION BY WISE MEN

PROPHECY OF SALVATION

W E BESEECH THEE, therefore, help Thy servants, whom Thou hast redeemed with Thy Precious Blood. « *3 times* »

RETURN TO NAZARETH

JESUS FOUND IN TEMPLE

33

Jesus, Mary, Joseph Hymn

(Melody of "Ave Maria" of Lourdes)

Hail JESUS, we pray Thee! O SAVIOR
    so good,
Assist us, Thy servants, redeemed by
    Thy Blood,
That Faith and Hope, with Love all divine,
May make our hearts more truly like
    Thine.
O MARY, our MOTHER, conceived with-
    out stain,
Benign Mediatrix in sorrow and pain,
Through Thy pure Heart, we offer our
    praise,
O lead us on in His Heart's meek ways.
St. JOSEPH, our PATRON, and friend
    of Christ's Heart,
Of Whose mystic Body, kind Guardian
    thou art,
May we abide, in His Heart beloved
As branch and vine, through His Precious
    Blood.

MEMORARE to JESUS, MARY, JOSEPH

REMEMBER, O Merciful Jesus, | Im-
maculate Mary | and glorious St.
Joseph | that no one has ever had recourse
to Your Protection, | or implored Your
assistance without obtaining relief. | Ani-
mated with a like confidence | but weighed
down by my sins, | I prostrate myself be-
fore You. | O! reject not my petitions, | but
graciously hear and grant them. Amen.

BENEDICTION PRAYER

O JESUS, Who hast said, | "Come to Me, and I will give you rest," | we have come, | heavily burdened with the cares and temptations of life. | Refresh us then, before we depart, | with Thy Holy Benediction, | so that carrying our cross with new hope and courage | till the end of life's pilgrimage, | we may be ready to hear from Thine Own Lips | those words of final Benediction, | "Come, blessed of My Father, | take possession of the kingdom prepared for you | from the foundation of the world." Amen.

Down in adoration falling
Lo! The sacred Host
we hail;
Lo! O'er ancient forms
departing
Newer rites of grace
prevail;
Faith for all defects
supplying
Where the feeble
senses fail.
To the everlasting Father
And the Son who reigns
on high

With the Spirit blest
proceeding,
Forth from each
eternally,
Be salvation, honor,
blessing,
Might, and endless
majesty. Amen
V You have given them
bread from heaven
(P.T. Alleluia)
R Having all sweetness
with it. (P.T. Alleluia)

At the Blessing look at Jesus and say, "My Lord and my God", or "May Thy Blessing come down upon me, O Lord! In the Name of the Father," etc.

RELIC of the TRUE CROSS is used at end of our service—a piece of the True Cross upon which Jesus shed His Precious Blood. As the priest blesses you at the Altar rail, say privately, "We beseech Thee," etc. Sing: "Holy God, We Praise Thy Name."

MY TRIPLE PRAYER

¶ *Most extraordinary graces have been received through the use of this prayer, which in one cry of confidence, directly and immediately calls upon Father, Son, Holy Spirit! and Jesus, Mary, Joseph!*

O Eternal **FATHER!** for the love of the Eternal Son, and for the love of the Eternal Holy Spirit, grant my request.

O Eternal **SON!** for the love of the Eternal Father, and for the love of the Eternal Holy Spirit, grant my request.

O Eternal **HOLY SPIRIT!** for the love of the Eternal Father and for the love of the Eternal Son, grant my request.

O my Crucified **JESUS,** for the love of the ever adorable Trinity, and for the love of Mary and Joseph, grant my request.

O **MARY,** my Mother, for the love of the ever adorable Trinity, and for the love of Jesus and Joseph, obtain my request.

O Holy **ST. JOSEPH,** for the love of the ever adorable Trinity, and for the love of Jesus and Mary, obtain my request.

ACT of CONFIDENCE

Heart of Jesus, I adore Thee,
Heart of Mary, I implore thee,
Heart of Joseph, meek and just,
In these three Hearts I place my trust.

NOVENA to the HOLY GHOST

O HOLY SPIRIT, make me faithful in every thought, and grant that I may always listen to Thy Voice, and watch for Thy Light, and follow Thy gracious Inspirations. I cling to Thee, and give myself to Thee, and ask Thee by Thy Compassion to watch over me in my weakness. « Holding the Pierced Feet of Jesus, looking at His Five Wounds, trusting in His Precious Blood, adoring His opened Side and stricken Heart « I implore Thee, Adorable Spirit, helper of my infirmity, to keep me in Thy Grace, now and always. Amen.

Act of RESIGNATION

L ORD, I know not what to ask; I merely present myself to Thee. Thou seest my miseries. Thou lovest me. Supply my needs according to Thy Mercy. I adore, without seeking to understand, Thy Holy Will. I resign myself to Thee, entirely and absolutely. I have no other desire but to do what Thou dost wish me to do. Teach me to pray, O Jesus! Pray within me Thyself. Amen.

NOVENA to our LADY of LOURDES

BE BLESSED, O most Pure Virgin, for having vouchsafed to manifest thyself shining with light, sweetness and beauty, in the grotto of Lourdes, saying to the child, St. Bernadette: "I am the IMMACULATE CONCEPTION" A thousand times we congratulate thee upon thine Immaculate Conception. Show that you are our Mother. Grant us ever to remember this great favor. Make us render to the Divine Goodness suitable thanksgiving. May the Church enjoy lasting peace and happiness.

O MARY IMMACULATE, inflame our hearts with one ray of the burning love of thy pure heart. Let them be consumed with love for Jesus and for thee, in order that we may more worthily congratulate thee here below and merit to congratulate thee one day in a glorious eternity. Amen.

ASPIRATION. A thousand times we congratulate thee, O Mary Immaculate; show thyself our Mother. « *One Our Father and Hail Mary* »

¶ *Recited at "Our Lady of Lourdes" Grotto at Monastery of Precious Blood; also during Novena from Feb. 2, feast of our Lady's Purification, to Feb. 11, feast of "Lady of Lourdes."*

Name your Novena Saint in this official prayer of the Church, when you wish to make a Novena to the Little Flower, St. Anne, St. Anthony, St. Francis Xavier, St. Gabriel, St. Jude, St. Rita, or to any favorite Saint.

May the Blessed Virgin Mary, Mother of God, and all the Saints intercede with God for us.

The Lord hath made His Saints wonderful. And heard them when they cried unto Him.

LET US PRAY

PRESERVE us, we beseech Thee, O Lord, from all dangers to soul and body, and by the intercession of the Blessed and Glorious Mary ever Virgin, Mother of God, « of St. Joseph, the holy Apostles Peter and Paul, of St. « *Name* » and all the Saints, « in Thy mercy, grant us health and peace, that after all adversity and error is removed, Thy Church may serve Thee in freedom and safety, through the same Jesus Christ, Thy Son, Our Lord, Who liveth and reigneth with Thee in the union of the Holy Spirit world without end. Amen.

St. « *Name* » pray for us. *Our Father, Hail Mary, Glory, etc.* « *3 times* »

MORNING PRAYERS

BAPTISM. The Sacrament by which I began a new day, receiving God's Own Life, when I was born again as a member of Christ's Mystical Body, the Church! cleansed from original sin, made a Christian, a child of God and an heir of Heaven! The new day when I took an oath of allegiance to serve under Christ, the King of all life.

(Always bless yourself on rising.)

✠ In the Name of the Father, and of the Son, and of the Holy Spirit. Amen.

(Our Father, Hail Mary, Glory be to the Father.)

O LORD GOD ALMIGHTY, Who hast safely brought us to the beginning of a new day, defend us this day by Thy Power, so that we may not only turn away from all sin, but also that our every thought, word and deed may proceed from and be directed according to Thy Will. Through our Lord Jesus Christ, Thy Son, Who liveth and reigneth with Thee in the union of the Holy Spirit, God world without end. Amen.

RENEWAL of BAPTISMAL VOWS

I RENEW my Baptismal Vows, I renounce Satan and all his works and all his pomps. I take JESUS CHRIST for my Model and my Guide and I promise to be faithful to Him unto the end of my life. Amen.

CONFIRMATION. *The Sacrament by which I received the Holy Spirit to make me a strong, perfect Christian and soldier of Jesus Christ; to fight Antichrist inside and outside myself; to be a co-worker with Christ in every form of Catholic Action.*

RENEWAL of CONFIRMATION GRACES

O MY GOD, I thank Thee for all Thy infinite Goodness in sending down upon my soul Thy Holy Spirit with all His Gifts and graces. O, may He take full possession of me forever. May His heavenly Wisdom reign in my heart; His Understanding enlighten my darkness; His Counsel guide me; His Fortitude strengthen me; His Knowledge instruct me; His Piety make me fervent; His Divine Fear keep me from all evil. Give me grace to be Thy faithful soldier, so that by fighting the good fight of faith, I may be brought to the crown of eternal life by the merits of Thy Son and our Savior, Jesus Christ. Amen.

EVENING PRAYERS

PENANCE. *The Sacrament by which, as a repentant sinner, I receive forgiveness even of mortal sin, and thus become again a living member of Christ's Mystical Body. Tonight, therefore, I shall examine my conscience in preparation for a full Confession, realizing that I must have a genuine sorrow for sin, together with a determination to sin no more.*

ETERNAL FATHER, I offer Thee the Sacred Heart of Jesus, with all Its Love, all Its sufferings and all Its merits:

TO EXPIATE all the sins I have committed this day, and during all my life. *Glory be to the Father, etc.*

TO PURIFY the good I have done in my poor way this day, and during all my life. *Glory be to the Father, etc.*

TO MAKE UP for the good I ought to have done and that I have neglected this day, and during all my life. *Glory be to the Father, etc.*

Recite Act of Contrition (page 50).

EXTREME UNCTION. Each night I should pray for this "Last Anointing" (however near or distant it may be). This Sacrament, received worthily, will insure my death in Christ's friendship. It is the greatest grace we can ask of God! A happy death means a Heaven of eternal happiness. A bad death means a Hell of eternal misery.

An ACT of RESIGNATION

MY LORD GOD, even now I accept at Thy hands, cheerfully and willingly, with all its anxieties, pains and sufferings, whatever kind of death it shall please Thee to be mine. Amen.

JESUS, MARY, JOSEPH, I give you my heart and my soul. JESUS, MARY, JOSEPH, assist me in my last agony. JESUS, MARY, JOSEPH, may I breathe forth my soul in peace with You. Amen.

PROTECTION DURING the NIGHT

VISIT, we beseech Thee, O Lord, this place, and drive far from it all snares of the enemy. May Thy holy Angels dwell herein to keep us in peace, and may Thy blessing be on us always. Amen.

COMMUNE with GOD DURING the DAY

HOLY EUCHARIST. Every one of us frequently thinks, speaks of God during each day, sometimes even taking His Name in vain. Develop the good habit of silent ejaculatory prayer. By such spiritual communing with God or by any simple aspiration of the soul, even a "prayer without words" while at work, during a temptation or while carrying a cross, you will thereby prepare for sacramental Communion. By this Sacrament of His very Body and Blood, His Soul and Divinity, Jesus satisfies man's instinctive hunger for a personal union with his God.

(Memorize, recite frequently during the day for your protection here, for your salvation hereafter.)

MY JESUS, mercy!
 . . . All for Thee, O most Sacred Heart of Jesus
Blessed be the Name of God

 . . . Grant, O Lord, that I may know Thy Will and do It
 . . . My God, I love Thee
 . . . O Jesus, save me
 . . . Sacred Heart of Jesus, I put my trust in Thee
 . . . Mother of Mercy, pray for us
 . . . Merciful Lord Jesus,

give them (him, her) everlasting rest

Join the Crusade for Purity.

Lust kills love, human and Divine. It is a chief cause of war here, misery hereafter.

BY THINE Immaculate Conception, O Mary, make my body pure and my soul holy. *Three times, followed each time by a Hail Mary.*

My Mother, keep me this day from mortal sin. *Hail Mary, three times.*

Gratitude for Daily Food.

BEFORE MEALS. Bless us, O Lord, and these Thy gifts, which we are about to receive from Thy bounty, and be Thou the eternal food of our souls, through Christ our Lord. Amen.

AFTER MEALS. We give Thee thanks, O Almighty God, for all Thy benefits, Who livest and reignest now and forever. Amen. May the souls of the faithful departed, through the mercy of God, rest in peace. Amen.

Wear your J. M. J. or Scapular Medal.

MATRIMONY. Jesus has promised to bless the house where an image of His Sacred Heart is exposed and honored. Once a week set a time, when the family gathers together, at mealtime or at Evening Prayers and recite this

CONSECRATION of FAMILY

 O JESUS, behold our family prostrate before Thee. Once more do we consecrate ourselves to Thee — our trials and joys—that our home, like Thine, may ever be the shrine of peace, purity, love, labor and faith. Do Thou protect and bless all of us, absent and present, living and dead.

O MARY, loving Mother of Jesus—and our Mother—pray to Jesus for our family, for all the families of the world, to guard the cradle of the newborn, the schools of the young and their vocations.

O JOSEPH, holy Guardian of Jesus and Mary, assist us by thy prayers in all the necessities of life. Ask of Jesus that special grace which He granted to thee, to watch over our home at the pillow of the sick and the dying, so that with Mary and with thee, Heaven may find our family unbroken in the Sacred Heart of Jesus. Amen.

Recite with family each first Friday.

OFFER SATURDAY for PRIESTS

HOLY ORDERS. Priests are messengers of God's Truth, dispensers of His Sacraments, announcers of Divine Law. They are ordained for your sake. For their sake, in union with Mary, Mother of the High Priest, give all of Saturday to God for His Priests.

DIVINE SAVIOR JESUS CHRIST, Who hast entrusted the whole work of Thy Redemption, the welfare and salvation of the world, to priests as Thy representatives, I offer Thee through the hands of Thy most holy Mother, all the prayers, works, sacrifices, joys and sorrows of this day for the sanctification of Thy priests.

GIVE US truly holy priests who seek nothing but Thy greater glory and the salvation of our souls. Bless their words and prayers at the altar, in the confessional, in the pulpit, in all their work for the young, the sick and the aged.

Do thou, O Mary, Mother of the High Priest, protect all priests from dangers to their holy vocation. Obtain for me a true spirit of faith and humble obedience so that I may ever behold the priest as the representative of God and willingly follow him in the Way, the Truth and the Life of Christ. Amen.

PREPARATION for CONFESSION

O MY GOD, grant me light to be truly sorry for my sins. To think that I have offended Thee after being forgiven so many times! I lay the rest of my life at Thy feet. How much more there is to come, I know not, but long or short, let it atone for my past.

Mary, my Mother, help me to make a good Confession.

¶ *Speak to the Priest as you would to our Lord Himself. Resolve to avoid deliberate sin and what leads to sin.*

When the Priest is ready, bless yourself and say, "Bless me, Father, for I have sinned. I confess to Almighty God, and to you, Father, that I have sinned. It is (how long) since my last Confession. Since then I have——"

RECONCILIATION

When ready, approach the priest for reconciliation. After being welcomed by the priest, make the sign of the cross with him. Once invited to trust in God for his mercy, listen to the word of God which proclaims mercy and calls man to conversion. Then in the light of God's Word, confess your sins seeking assistance from the priest if necessary.

CONFESSION–EXAMINE CONSCIENCE
In My DUTIES to GOD

Neglecting Morning or Evening Prayers ... Superstitious practices ... Consulting fortunetellers ... Receiving Sacraments sacrilegiously ... Against FAITH by wilful doubts concerning any article of the Creed, or by reading or circulating irreligious books ... Against HOPE by despair, murmuring or presuming on God's Mercy ... Against CHARITY by wilfully rebellious thoughts against God or His Law, or by omitting good works through fear of others.

Irreverence towards God, His Name, His Church ... Cursing or swearing ... False, unlawful and unnecessary oaths ... Breaking lawful vows ... Neglecting Mass on Sundays and holydays, or performing unrequired servile work.

In My DUTIES to My NEIGHBOR

Insulting or neglecting parents ... Failing to send children to religious schools when possible . . . Bad example . . . Neglecting home, trade, professional, civil service duties . . . Ignoring the Spiritual and Corporal Works of Mercy ... Any violent act ... Causing hard feeling ... Revenge ... Refusing re-

concilation . . . Inducing others to sin
. . . Stealing (what value or damage?)
. . . Possession of ill-gotten goods . . .
Cheating . . . Culpable delay in paying
lawful debts . . . Lying . . . Perjury . . .
Fraud . . . Slander, detraction or rash
judgments . . . Failure to support my
Church . . . Also examine your con-
science according to Works of Mercy.

In RELATION to MYSELF

Obstinacy . . . Sloth . . . Desiring or
yielding to sensuality, impurity, glut-
tony, drunkenness . . . Rage, envy,
impatience, jealousy . . . Failure to fast
or abstain . . . Failure to make my
Easter Duty . . . Waste of time, money
or talents.

LORD JESUS CHRIST, you are
the Lamb of God; you take away
the sins of the world. Through the
grace of the Holy Spirit restore me to
friendship with your Father, cleanse
me from every stain of sin in the blood
you shed for me, and raise me to new
life for the glory of your name.

Act of PERFECT CONTRITION

O MY GOD, I am heartily sorry and beg pardon for all my sins NOT SO MUCH because these sins bring suffering and Hell to me » but because they have crucified my loving Savior Jesus Christ and offended Thy Infinite Goodness. I firmly resolve, with the help of Thy grace, to confess my sins, to do penance and to amend my life. Amen.

« Or as ejaculation say frequently »

O MY GOD, I am sorry for having offended Thee, because I love Thee.

¶ *Perfect Contrition becomes easy by meditating on a Crucifix: "Who" is suffering? "What" is He suffering? "Why?" To be sorry in one's feelings is not necessary; it is sufficient if the will turns from sin to the love of God.*

¶ *Teach the Act of Perfect Contrition to non-Catholics » especially to one in danger of death. Form the habit of making it yourself. It can save your soul at death if no priest is near for the last Sacraments.*

Preparing to "RECEIVE"

Question. What about my "favorite" Communion Prayers?

Answer. These other "preparation" prayers (pages 53 to 57) should not be recited during Mass . . . but before Mass begins.

Question. Why are the Mass Prayers the best way for preparing to "receive"?

Answer No. 1. Because the official Mass Prayers, such as the priest himself recites, prepare us to "give" ourselves with Jesus to the Father—and then "receive" the gift of Jesus from the Father.

Answer No. 2. Because these Mass Prayers contain within themselves all the "acts" of this or that "virtue" necessary to "receive" worthily.

Question. What "Acts before Communion" are contained in the Mass Prayers?

Answer. The Mass Prayers include the

Act of Contrition —from the beginning to Kyrie;

Act of Faith —from the Prayer to Creed;

Act of Hope —from the Offertory to "Our Father": that the gift of ourselves when united with Jesus will be "received" by the Father.

Act of Love —awaiting the Gift of Love in holy union with God.

Act of Gratitude and a plea for perseverance—to the end of Holy Mass.

BEFORE COMMUNION
Recite before, not during Mass.

MOTHER MARY, you who pre-
pared the first resting-place for
God on earth « who prepared the man-
ger for Him on Christmas night « and
your own pure heart again and again
to receive Him in Holy Communion
« prepare mine for Him, now. Make
haste, dear Mother, for the time is short.
Would that I had the heart and love for
God and neighbor with which thou didst
communicate. Give me this morning thy
Jesus, as thou didst give Him to the shepherds and the kings.

I receive Him from thy most pure hands.
Tell Him I am your baptized child and
His confirmed soldier « thus He will look
upon me with a more Loving Eye, and
when He comes He will press me more
closely to His Sacred Heart. Amen.

Prayer by an Old Lady

Recite before, not during Mass.

"**M**Y LOVING LORD, a thousand welcomes! O Son of Mary, I love You, indeed I do. Who am I at all that You should come next or near me? O God of Heaven! make a little corner for me in Your Heart, and never, while there's life in me, let me lose my place there, and after death may I still hide there. Amen."

"Have pity on me, O Blessed Mother! Talk to my God for me. Tell Him I'm a poor ignorant creature, full of nothing but sin and misery; but that I love you, His Own dear Mother; and that I am a poor follower of Him, and for your sweet sake, to help and pity me. Amen."

BEFORE COMMUNION

Recite before, not during Mass.

COME, O JESUS! My poor soul calls for Thee and awaits Thee. Comfort my poor soul distressed. Come and dwell within my breast. My Savior, Jesus, come to me. With all my heart I long for Thee. Most firmly I believe in Thee. Most truthfully I hope in Thee. Most ardently I love

Thee. Then come, O Jesus, come to me.

Let me receive Thy BODY, so weary with suffering, so tortured to save me. Let me receive Thy Blood, Which agony for me pressed from Thy Brow in the Garden and Which Thou didst shed for love of me, every step of the Way of Thy Cross.

Let me receive Thy SOUL, so sweet, and strong, meek and compassionate. Let It lift my soul to Thee.

Come, dear Jesus, with Thy DIVINITY. Print Thy Divine Image on my soul, and make it holy through Thy grace.

Every day I need Thy LIGHT to guide me in the way God wants me to go. Come, then, O my Host, and day by day enlighten my soul with Thy Divine Grace.

Jesus in the Host! GIVES *His Life! when I* RECEIVE

Jesus in the Host! RECEIVES *my life when I* GIVE

Every day I need Thy STRENGTH to fulfill God's reason for my creation. Come, O my Host, and give me strength to set aside every obstacle in following Thee.

In my trials and afflictions of every day, come, O my Host, and give me patience and resignation.

In the duties and obligations which every day brings, come, O my Host, and give me strength to be faithful to them.

Every day I ought to do good about me, to set good example to my neighbors, perhaps to console and counsel them. Come, then, O my Host, day by day, and inspire me with Thy Divine Charity.

Every day is full of temptations and I am weak. Come, O my Host, and day by day renew my powers; raise me up from my falls; purify me from my faults.

O JESUS, when dawns the day which shall be my last, come to me as my Divine Friend. Come to me as my Host for the last time on earth « so that, having begun every day of my life on earth with Thee, I may also begin the day of eternity that shall never end with Thee. Amen.

RECEIVING HOLY COMMUNION

¶ *In going to the Altar rail and returning to your place, keep your hands joined « your eyes cast down « your thoughts on Jesus Christ.*

St. John "receives" at the Last Supper.
Pictured in Sanctuary of our Chapel

HOLY COMMUNION

After HOLY COMMUNION

JESUS, His Body and Blood, remains within you at least 15 minutes . . . a time for communing with Him by reciting slowly some of the following prayers after Mass (pages 58 to 67).

Prayer Before a CRUCIFIX

GOOD and sweetest Jesus, before Thy Face I humbly kneel, and with the greatest fervor of spirit I pray and beseech Thee to fix deep in my heart lively sentiments of faith, hope and charity, true sorrow for my sins and a firm purpose of amendment « whilst I consider Thy five most Precious Wounds, having before my eyes, the words of David, the Prophet, concerning Thee, my Jesus: "They have pierced My Hands and My Feet, they have numbered all My Bones" « *Our Father, Hail Mary, Glory be, etc., for Holy Father's intentions,*

O MOST HOLY GOD, I adore Thee, through the Adorable Sacrament of the Altar, and I offer Thee, through the holy hands of the Immaculate Virgin Mary, all the consecrated Hosts on our Altars as a sacrifice of expiation, reparation, and atonement for all the sacrileges, profanations, impieties, blasphemies, and crimes committed against Thee throughout the universe.

Act of REPARATION

O GOOD JESUS, in gratitude for Thy many Graces, and in sorrow for many abuses of these Graces, I wish at this moment, both for myself, ever ungrateful, and for the world, ever criminal, to make an Act of Solemn Reparation. Listen then, O merciful Savior of our souls, listen to these Acts of Faith, to these expressions of sorrow:

For the irreverence we have committed in the House of God « *I wish to make reparation.*

For our careless and distracted attendance at Sunday Mass « *I wish, etc.* . . . .

For our lack of preparation before, and our poor thanksgiving after Holy Communion « *I wish to make reparation.*

For our failure to co-operate with Thy daily Graces « *I wish to make reparation.*

For our sins of pride, sensuality and of our entire life « *I wish, etc.* . . . .

For our bad example and the sins we have caused in others « *I wish, etc.* . . . .

For our tragic indifference to Thy words of Holy Scripture and to the words of our Holy Father the Pope « *I wish, etc.* . . . .

For the deplorable untruths of heresy, for all deserters and apostates « *I wish to make reparation.*

For the pleasure-seeking and money-mad profaners of the Lord's Day « *I wish to make reparation.*

For the sacrilegious treatment of Thy Churches and Altars « *I wish, etc. . . .*

For the diabolical agents of Hell, ever seeking whom they may devour « *I wish to make reparation.*

For the heartbreaking outrages committed by those who should be Thy greatest consolation « *I wish to make reparation.*

"O Love neglected! O Goodness but too little known."

WHAT SHALL I GIVE THEE?

« *After Communion Prayer* »
Recite after, not during Mass.

I HAVE RECEIVED into my heart, Jesus Christ, His Body and Blood, Soul and Divinity! I begin this day as a day in Heaven. He is in my soul « the Divine Infant in the crib « the growing Boy at Nazareth « the Apostle acclaimed by crowds on the roads of Galilee « the Miracle Worker Who performed such prodigies « the Martyr Who completed His Sacrifice on Calvary.

He is in me « What more can I desire when I possess Jesus?

And now, O good Master! what shall I give Thee in exchange for Thy visit . . . ? I would like to give Thee a soul all sparkling with purity and sincerity, but mine is afflicted with so many miseries!

I would like to pray to Thee with the burning words of Thy Mother and her court of Heaven, but I feel riveted to earthly things . . .

I would like to offer Thee courageous loyalty to my Baptismal Vows and Confirmation Graces, but, alas, I have so often been disloyal . . .

I would like, at least, to have a desire for the Christian life, but I allow myself to be discouraged by my failures . . .

O good Jesus! I have nothing to give Thee, and Thou hast given Everything; Thou hast given Thyself to me. I can only join my poor voice in the chorus of praise to Thee, rising out of all the works of Thy Creation here on earth . . .

With the majesty of the mountains, the immensity of the desert, the roar of the ocean, the fury of the storm, *I shall praise Thy Power!*

With the flowers of the field, the colors of the rainbow, the whiteness of the snow, the blue of the skies, *I shall praise Thy Beauty!*

With the fruits of the earth, the air I breathe, the light I see, the life I enjoy, *I shall praise Thy Goodness.*

With the splendor of the stars, the rays of the sun, the moon's pale light, the depths of space, *I shall praise Thine Immensity.*

With fifteen hundred millions now living on earth, *I shall praise Thy Mercy!* May our voices unite with the billions of those who inhabited the earth before us, and out of whose dust the beauty of nature perpetually rises to *praise Thy Glory!*

May an infinite concert of voices from cottages and palaces, from fields and forests, from towns and deserts, from workshops and cathedrals, from earth and from heaven, from time and from eternity, arise to give my thanks unto Thee! Amen.

MY QUEEN! my Mother! I give thee all myself, and, to show my devotion to thee, I consecrate to thee this day, my eyes, ears, mouth, heart, my entire self. Wherefore, O good Mother, since I am thine own, keep me, defend me, as thy property and possession.

The TWELVE PROMISES

Based on Promises to St. Margaret Mary.

O HEART OF JESUS, behold us prostrate before Thee, to adore Thee,
to praise Thee, to thank Thee, to make
reparation for our past faults, and to
consecrate ourselves to Thy Love.
Bearing in mind Thy magnificent Promises to those who honor and love Thy
Sacred Heart, we say to Thee with the
utmost confidence:

1 » Heart of Jesus, give us all the graces
necessary for our state in life. *Thou hast
promised it, O Jesus!*

2 » Heart of Jesus, grant peace to our
families. *Thou hast promised it, etc.*

3 » Heart of Jesus, console us in all our
sorrows. *Thou hast promised it, O Jesus!*

4 » Heart of Jesus, be our safe Refuge
our death, and above all at the hour of
Thou hast promised it, etc.

5 » Heart of Jesus, pour abundant blessings on all our labors. *Thou hast promised
it, O Jesus!*

6 » Heart of Jesus, be for sinners the
Source and Infinite Ocean of Mercy.
Thou hast promised it, O Jesus!

7 » Heart of Jesus, make indifferent souls
fervent. *Thou hast promised it, O Jesus!*

8 » Heart of Jesus, make fervent souls advance rapidly to perfection. *Thou hast promised it, O Jesus!*

9 » Heart of Jesus, bless the houses where Thine Image is exposed and honored. *Thou hast promised it, O Jesus!*

10 » Heart of Jesus, give to priests the power of touching the most hardened hearts. *Thou hast promised it, O Jesus!*

11 » Heart of Jesus, engrave on Thy Heart forever the names of those who propagate this devotion. *Thou hast promised it, O Jesus!*

12 » Heart of Jesus, give those who RE-CEIVE HOLY COMMUNION NINE CONSEC-UTIVE FIRST FRIDAYS, the grace of final repentance, that they may not die under Thy displeasure, but, strengthened by the reception of the Sacraments, may Thy Heart be their secure refuge at their last hour. *Thou hast promised it, O Jesus!*

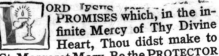

ORD JESUS, recall the PROMISES which, in the infinite Mercy of Thy Divine Heart, Thou didst make to St. Margaret Mary. Be the PROTECTOR of our life; the STRENGTH of our weakness; the REPAIRER of our faults; the COMPLETION of our virtues; our REFUGE at the hour of our death. Amen.

CONSECRATION to JESUS

O JESUS, be pleased to receive my poor offering. Thou hast given Thyself to me. I want to give myself to Thee, unworthy as I am.

I give Thee MY BODY that in Thee it may be kept chaste and pure.

I give Thee MY SOUL that Thou mayest keep it clean from every stain of sin.

I give Thee MY EVERY THOUGHT, WORD AND ACT for the intentions of Thy Sacred Heart.

I give Thee MYSELF in life and in death, that I may be Thine forever. Amen.

EJACULATORY PRAYER

¶ *is a practical form of prayer which should appeal to the busy and distracted modern mind.*

¶ *Why should I not speak to God during my busy day with brief ejaculations?*

¶ *Frequently say:*

"My Jesus, mercy"

to purge my soul of lesser sins and faults . . . or

"Grant, O Lord, that I may know Thy will and do it"   *to illumine my soul . . . or*

"Sweet Heart of Jesus, be my Love"
                         to unite my soul with God.

A CONTRACT with JESUS

O JESUS! my Savior, I desire above all things to show my love for Thee and for my neighbor, loved by Thee; to praise Thee as far as lies within my power and to make Thy Kingdom come amongst men. Therefore, I make the following contract. I shall try to remain faithful to it to the end of my life.

Whereas: FIRST » I propose in my EVERY LOOK to consecrate myself entirely to Thee, to see Thee through the eyes of faith, in all creatures and in all things of earth.

SECOND » I propose in EVERY THROB OF MY HEART to prove that I love Thee enough to detach myself from sin and its occasions; and in all my human loves to love them through Thee.

THIRD » I propose that EVERY BREATH I breathe shall be in praise of Thee, my Giver of Eternal Life. O, breathe Thy Grace abundantly upon my heart, and on all men's hearts, thereby to establish Thy Reign amongst us.

FOURTH » I propose, finally, O my Jesus, in every act of my soul and in every action

of my body, to unite with Thee in Thy
Sacrifice of love on Calvary and in Thy
continued Sacrifice in all the Masses that
have been, are being, or will be celebrated
« all the merits of Thy Passion and Death
« and the merits for all of us in the holy
life and sufferings of Thy Blessed Mother
and of all the Saints. Accept these offer-
ings, O Merciful Jesus, in adoration of
Thy Divine Majesty, as reparation for all
sins « as thanksgiving for all of God's gifts
and graces « for the conversion of infidels
and sinners « for the perseverance of the
just and the deliverance of the souls in
Purgatory.

O JESUS, deign to accept and confirm this
contract. Amen.

OFFERING of ONESELF

ACCEPT, O Lord, this offering of
my liberty, memory, understanding and will. All that I am and
have, Thou hast given me. I want to
restore everything to Thee, O Lord.
Dispose of me as it shall please Thee.
All that I ask is Thy Grace and Thy
Love. With these alone I shall be rich
enough. I ask for nothing more.

Come to Me . . . you burdened
I will give you rest

¶ *You believe, of course, that Jesus is really present in whatever church you may be near every day.*

¶ *But do you act on this belief? "What greater friend have you than Jesus, Brother, Savior, Physician, Advocate?"*

¶ *Do you know that "visiting a friend to talk things over" is the oldest social custom; begun by God Himself on a visit to our first parents; but, sad to say, even as we, they "hid themselves"; that God cried out then, even as now, "Where art thou?" (Genesis 3:9.)*

¶ *Do you not recall how Jesus, as soon as He was born, sent heavenly Angels to nearby Shepherds, and by a heavenly star directed the three Wise Men from afar, to visit Him?*

¶ *Do you realize that the Same Mind, the Same Heart, the Same Hands are in the Tabernacle to counsel you, to befriend you, to bless you! Do you "realize"?*

To Our LADY of the BLESSED SACRAMENT

O VIRGIN MARY, Our Lady of the Blessed Sacrament, glory of the Christian people; joy of the universal Church; salvation of the world; pray for us, and arouse among the faithful everywhere such devotion to the Most Holy Eucharist, as will make them worthy to receive It every day.

To JESUS ABANDONED in TABERNACLE

¶ *Ask Mary, who was entirely faithful to Jesus in His earthly life, when He was the tortured object of so much ignorance, indifference, defiance,*
¶ *Ask Mary to direct your prayers to some neglected or abandoned Tabernacle somewhere in the world.*
¶ *Spread the word about this devotion to others, so that there may be not one Abandoned Tabernacle in the whole world.*

WITH Mary Immaculate, let us adore, thank, implore and console the Most Beloved and Sacred Heart of Jesus in the Blessed Sacrament.

O DIVINE JESUS! lonely tonight in so many Tabernacles, without visitor or worshipper . . . I offer Thee my poor heart. May its every throb be an act of Love for Thee! Thou art always watching beneath the Sacramental Veils « in Thy Love Thou dost never sleep and Thou art never weary of Thy vigil for sinners. O lonely Jesus! May the flame of my heart burn and beam always in company with Thee. O Sacrament most Holy! O Sacrament Divine! All praise and all thanksgiving be every moment Thine!

To JESUS FORSAKEN

Sweet Jesus! For how many ages hast Thou hung upon Thy Cross and still men pass Thee by and regard Thee not!

How often have I passed Thee by, heedless of Thy great Sorrow, Thy many Wounds, Thy infinite Love!

How often have I stood before Thee, not to comfort and console Thee, but to add to Thy Sorrows, to deepen Thy Wounds, to spurn Thy Love!

Thou hast stretched forth Thy Hands to raise me up, and I have taken those Hands and bent them back on the Cross.

Thou hast loved me with an infinite love, and I have taken advantage of that love to sin the more against Thee.

My ingratitude has pierced Thy Sacred Heart, and Thy Heart responds only with an outpouring of Thy Love in Thy Precious Blood.

Lamb of God, Who takest away the sins of the world, have mercy on me.

FAITH in the REAL PRESENCE

WE COME to Thee, dear Lord, like the Apostles, saying: "IN-CREASE OUR FAITH." Give us a VIVID FAITH, that Thou art really present in the Blessed Sacrament « a STRONG and ACTIVE FAITH that we may live by it.

Give us the FAITH of Thy beloved disciple, John, to recognize Thee and say: "It is the Lord." "My God and my All!"

Give us the FAITH of Peter to fall on our knees and confess: "Thou art the Christ, the Son of the Living God."

Give us the FAITH of Mary Magdalen to fall at Thy Feet, crying, "Rabboni, Master!"

Give us the FAITH of the father of the sick boy « that FAITH which You rewarded with a miracle when he cried out in tears, "I do believe, Lord! help my unbelief."

Give us the FAITH of all Thy Saints to whom the Blessed Sacrament was Heaven begun on earth. In every Communion and at every visit, increase our FAITH, our LOVE, our HUMILITY, our REVERENCE, and all good things will come to us. Dearest Lord, INCREASE OUR FAITH.

Why callest thou Me?

¶ *Carved by an unknown sculptor, into the walls of an old European Cathedral, this appeal expresses the grief of Christ.*

Thou callest Me MASTER . . .
                yet heedest not Me,
Thou callest Me LIGHT . . .
                yet I shine not in thee.
Thou callest Me WAY . . .
                but dost follow Me not,
Thou callest Me LIFE . . .
                yet My Name is forgot.
Thou callest Me TRUTH . . .
                but playest a false role,
Thou callest Me GUIDE . . .
                yet despisest control.
Thou callest Me LOVING . . .
                withholding thy heart,
Thou callest Me RICH . . .
                yet desirest no part.
Thou callest Me GOOD . . .
                and yet evil thy ways,
Thou callest Me ETERNAL . . .
                while wasting thy days.
Thou callest Me NOBLE . . .
                yet draggest Me down,
Thou callest Me MIGHTY . . .
                not fearing My frown.
Thou callest Me JUST . . .
                oh! if just then I be,
When I shall condemn thee,
                reproach thou not Me.

CATHOLIC ACTION

¶ *Nowhere can we better learn the twofold duty of Catholic Action than before the Blessed Sacrament, where Jesus satisfies man's hunger for a personal union with God. "He who eats My Flesh . . . abides in Me, and I in him"; secondly, where Jesus unites men together in a real social and mystical union, to work for one another, since "we though many, are one body, all of us who partake of the one Bread."*

O LORD JESUS, Who hast said, "By this will all men know that you are my disciples, if you have love for one another," grant us, we beseech Thee, an active share in Thine Own zeal for souls. If I had not been redeemed by Thee, where would I be at this moment? What bewildering questions and doubts would now be afflicting my soul if Thou hadst not given me the light of faith? Save me, O Jesus, from that blinding indifference, praying and acting merely for my own needs, while, at my own door, amongst my own acquaintances there are so many starved minds in need of Thy Truth; so many famished hearts in need of Thy Love. Have mercy on me, O Jesus, and grant me the grace to rise from my slumber, and fix deep in my soul such a personal love for Thee that I may act always and everywhere for the salvation of other souls, especially in those works recommended by our Holy Father, our Bishops and Pastors. Amen.

To the DIVINE PRISONER

« *For a Visit* »

O JESUS, DIVINE PRISONER « present always in the Tabernacle as a ransom for my sins « look on me « a prisoner too « bound by my own guilt. O, relieve me from the shackles of my sins « that I may give myself to the service of Thy Love.

Deliver me from the shackles of my pride, sweet Jesus « from my vanity, sloth and anger « melt the stiffness of my will, break the tyranny of my passions « open wide the door of my dungeoned soul and dispel the darkness of my sins and ignorance.

Have pity, O Divine Prisoner! Have pity on this poor prisoner. Help me to escape from sin so that I may always be with Thee . . . forever Thy prisoner! My mind chained by Thy Truth! My will chained by Thy Law! My heart chained by Thy Love! Chain me to Thee, living and dying. And may I die, dear Jesus, a prisoner in Thy Sacred Heart. Amen.

REPARATION

JESUS, my Savior, True God and True Man, with my whole heart I love Thee. « I adore Thee in the most august Sacrament of the Altar, in reparation for any irreverence I have ever shown Thee « profaning Thy Sacred Name « desecrating Thy Holy Altars « and for all such acts done by others and that yet may be done I implore Thy forgiveness.

I adore Thee, my God, not indeed as Thou deservest nor as much as I am bound to adore, but as far as I am able. Would that I could adore Thee with all the perfection of which a reasonable creature is capable. Meantime, I purpose now and ever to adore Thee; not only for those Catholics who adore and love Thee not, but also for the conversion of all bad Christians; of all heretics, schismatics, Mohammedans, Jews and idolaters.

JESUS, my God, mayest Thou be ever known, adored, loved and praised every moment, in the most Holy and Divine Sacrament. Amen.

TRUST HIM when dark doubts assail thee « trust Him when thy strength is small « trust Him when to simply trust Him « seems the hardest thing of all.

PLEA

JESUS of the Eucharist! Come to us and be our Ruler. All that we have and are is Thine to command, for all that we have is Thine. If our hearts are poor, enrich them with Thy Grace. If they have been wretched and stained, accept them purged and cleansed through the Immaculate Heart of Mary.

SUFFERING HEART of Jesus! To Thee we confide all the trials of our souls.

SWEET HEART of Jesus! To Thy care we confide our weaknesses and ask Thee to accept our sincere repentance.

COMPASSIONATE HEART of Jesus! We confide our souls to Thee, tormented by our suffering conscience.

GENTLE HEART of Jesus! We confide to Thee the peace and salvation of our families.

EUCHARISTIC HEART of Jesus! The world, worried unto death, finds a refuge in Thy Heart, where the lance once opened for us the source of Life.

Come, O Jesus! Be our Brother in the pure joy of Christian love!

Come, O Jesus! Be our Friend in the depths of this world's sorrows.

To JESUS CHRIST, KING

O CHRIST JESUS, I acknowledge Thee as Universal King. All that has been made, was created for Thee. Exercise over me all the rights that Thou hast.

I renew my Baptismal Promises, renouncing Satan, his pomps and his works, and I promise to live as a good Christian « Especially do I pledge myself, by all the means in my power, to bring about the triumph of the rights of God and of Thy Church.

DIVINE HEART of Jesus, I consecrate all my poor actions to the cause of Thy Kingship, that all hearts may recognize Thee their Ruler and thus establish the Kingdom of Thy Peace in all the world. Amen.

*Dear Lord, I pray Thy
  Hand to take
My body, broken now
  for Thee!
Accept the sacrifice
  I make
Oh! Body, broken once
  for me!*

HAIL, CHRIST, OUR KING

MOST SWEET JESUS! Come near to us, Thy children. Receive from our hands that crown which those who are but dust of earth, try to seize from Thee. Enter now in triumph among us, Thy fervent followers! «Hail, Christ, our King!

Lawmakers may break the tables of Thy Law, but whilst they lose their thrones and are forgotten, we, Thy subjects, will continue to salute Thee «Hail, Christ, our King!

They have said that Thy GOSPEL is out-of-date, that it hinders progress, and must no longer be considered. They who say this soon disappear into obscurity and are forgotten; whilst we, who adore Thee, continue to salute Thee «Hail, Christ, our King!

The proud, the worldly « those who possess

unlawful riches « those who thirst for riches, honors and pleasures alone « declaring Thy moral law to be for past ages « will be hurled against the Rock of Calvary and Thy Church and falling, will be reduced to dust, and sink into oblivion, « whilst we, Thy followers, continue to salute Thee « Hail, Christ, our King!

Those who seek the dawn of a material civilization, divorced from God, will surely die, poisoned by their own false doctrine, deserted and cursed by their own children « whilst we, who would console Thee, will continue to salute Thee « Hail, Christ, our King!

Yes, hail to Thee, O Christ, our King! Put to flight Lucifer, the fallen angel of darkness, from our homes, schools and society « force him and his agents into Hell « chain him there everlastingly « whilst we, Thy friends, continue to salute Thee « Hail, Christ, our King!

Prayer for COURAGE

DEAREST LORD, teach me to be generous, teach me to serve Thee as Thou deservest « to give and not to count the cost « to fight and not to heed the wound « to toil and not to seek for rest « to labor and not to seek reward, save that of feeling that I do Thy Will « *St. Ignatius* »

*TODAY'S LIVING WAY of the CROSS

"If anyone wishes to come after me, let him take up his cross daily." (Luke 9; 23)

¶ The Way of the Cross is not finished. Along Calvary Road we all come . . . He beckons the Pope, His representative, your Bishop . . . priests and nuns close to Him and us . . . all cross-carriers!

¶ Old age stoops along with piled-up burdens . . . then parish priests point the way to employer, laborers . . . Christ looks down the line to the fallen one . . . "Take courage, do not be afraid." (Matt. 14; 27)

¶ Youth comes along . . . never will cross seem so light . . . mother follows sorrowfully . . . her little girl sees the world as a big happy playground . . . but her cross, a paralyzed limb, begins to weigh her down.

¶ All cross-bearers . . . the shadow of New York's giant sky-line falls over the scene. In what spirit do I carry my cross? It will be lighter if I follow the Leader.

*Painting (each 100 feet long) on Epistle and Gospel side walls of Precious Blood Monastery, Brooklyn, N. Y.

EXCHANGED for PALM of ETERNAL PEACE

"Come, take possession of the kingdom prepared for you." (Matt. 25; 34)

¶ It is easy to picture "Today's Living Way of the Cross." It is visible all around us. But how paint the now invisible Heaven!

¶ "Eye has not seen nor ear heard what things God has prepared." (1 Cor. 2; 9)

¶ "And death shall be no more; neither shall there be pain any more." (Apoc. 21; 4). Behold, we exchange cross of suffering for palm of victory . . . Pope, as a spiritual father, at the rear, making sure of his children's entry . . . the little child first.

¶ All enter through Christ's Church, symbolized by dome of St. Peter's Basilica . . . all receive the "crown of justice, which the Lord will give to those who love his coming." 2 Tim. 4; 8)

¶ "We see now in an obscure manner, but then face to Face" (1 Cor. 13; 12) . . . faith yielding to Vision . . . love being perfected in Union with God. Do I now live by hope?

JESUS, HELP ME!

IN EVERY need let me come to Thee with humble trust, saying « Jesus, help me! In all my doubts, perplexities, and temptations « Jesus, help me!

In hours of loneliness, weariness and trials « Jesus, help me!

In the failure of my plans and hopes; in disappointments, troubles and sorrows « Jesus, help me!

When others fail me, and Thy Grace alone can assist me « Jesus, help me!

When I throw myself on Thy Tender Love as a Father and Savior « Jesus, help me!

When my heart is cast down by failure, at seeing no good come from my efforts « Jesus, help me!

When I feel impatient, and my cross irritates me « Jesus, help me!

When I am ill, and my head and hands cannot work and I am lonely « Jesus, help me!

Always, always, in spite of weakness, falls and shortcomings of every kind « Jesus, help me and never forsake me.

« Composed by an English Bishop during his last illness. »

THY KINGDOM COME

LORD, we ask for more than Thy Mercy! We desire Thee to reign over us. Thine interests must be ours. « By the Love of Thy Sacred Heart, which surpasses all knowledge, we beg Thee, O Jesus, to fulfill in our time the promises made to St. Margaret Mary. In union with Holy Church, through the intercession of Thy Virgin Mother, for the honor of Thy Holy Name, JESUS, we ask Thee to hasten and establish the reign of Thy Divine Heart, here and now.

Triumph by the reign of Thy Sacred Heart! Hasten Thy reign, O Jesus, before Satan and the world snatch more souls from Thee and corrupt every state of life.

Triumph by the reign of Thy Sacred Heart! Come, O Jesus! and gain the victory of Thy Love in every home. Reign there by Thy Peace, promised to all who have joyfully received Thee into their homes.

Triumph by the reign of Thy Sacred Heart! « Do not delay, Beloved Jesus, for many homes are suffering bitter evils which Thou alone canst heal.

Triumph by the reign of Thy Sacred Heart! « Come! because Thou art strong; because Thou art the God of life's battles. In Thy Pierced and Wounded Side is Thy Pledge to us and our hope of Heaven at the hour of death.

Triumph by the reign of Thy Sacred Heart! « Good Master! what of the numberless lukewarm and indifferent souls? Hasten to enlighten them in devotion to Thy Loving Heart.

Triumph by the reign of Thy Sacred Heart! « Give to priests who love Thee, and who preach Thy Love « the power of eloquence to draw souls to Thy Heart.

Triumph by the reign of Thy Sacred Heart! « Finally, Lord Jesus, grant that by our fidelity to FIRST FRIDAY COMMUNION, we may obtain the rewards of THY GREAT PROMISE « the grace that we shall not die under Thy displeasure, nor without receiving the last Sacraments « that Thy Divine Heart may be our final refuge at that last hour.

Ask Our LORD'S BLESSING
Before leaving the Blessed Sacrament.

BLESS ME, O God of bounty! Bless me, Thou Who art holy and good! Bless me as Thou didst bless the patriarchs and prophets; as Thou didst bless Thy beloved Mother; as Thou didst bless Thy disciples before ascending into Heaven.

BLESS MY EYES. Never permit them to behold vanity. BLESS MY EARS. Set around them a hedge of thorns to guard them from hearing unchristian words. BLESS MY MOUTH. Surround it with a guard of truth and kindness. BLESS MY BODY. Grant that chastity may clothe it as with a garment of glory. BLESS MY MIND. Grant that my thoughts may be like Thine. BLESS MY HEART. Kindle in it the fire of love which Thou didst bring on earth. Make it the sanctuary of every virtue.

ST. TERESA'S BOOKMARK
« *A Volume of Wisdom in itself* »

Let nothing disturb thee,
Let nothing affright thee.
All things are passing;
God only is changeless.
Patience gains all things.
Who hath God wanteth nothing,
Alone God sufficeth.

The SEVEN BLOODSHEDDINGS

The Christian life is traced out in the SEVEN Bloodsheddings of our Lord.

One a day sanctifies entire week

"**B**Y THE MERITS of Thy Precious Blood, shed seven times, keep me ever united to Thee; save me at death from the agonizing memory of a wasted life." « *Recite at each Shedding* »

I. THE CIRCUMCISION

FOR SUNDAY

calls me to a life of union with God « "Abide in Me and I in you!" Jesus receives His Name in a Baptism of Blood. He shares in our human life that I may share in His Divine Life.

II. THE AGONY IN THE GARDEN

FOR MONDAY

shows sin as the destroyer of our life of union with God. Jesus sweated Blood because He foresaw me rejecting Him for sin « My many sins crushed His Bleeding Heart.

III. THE SCOURGING

warns me against being separated from union with God, forever in Hell. As my Savior He suffers scourges « instead of me who deserves them » to save me from the scourges of sin, both in this world and in Hell.

FOR TUESDAY

IV. THE CROWNIN WITH THORNS

counsels mental prayer as the first means of preserving my life of union with God. Spiky thorns almost scalped His Head. As they crowned Him Fool and bent the knee before Him in mock prayer and worship, what mental suffering our Lord endured.

FOR WEDNESDAY

V. THE CARRYING OF THE CROSS

emphasizes patience in carrying my cross through life, as the second means of keeping my life of union with God. His Cross crushed Him to the ground. Old Wounds were widened. New Wounds were opened in His Hands

FOR

THURSDAY

and Knees. To carry my cross patiently in union with His, is my best penance for past sin and the best protection against future sin.

VI. THE CRUCIFIXION urges: never give up the ideal of a life united with God.

FOR FRIDAY

Jesus now clings to His Eternal Ideal. When I am tempted to give up my old ideals of prayer, sacrifice and purity, I must plead with Him to raise these dead ideals to life.

VII. THE PIERCING OF THE HEART inspires me to final perseverance in my life of union with God.

FOR SATURDAY

His Love for me persevered until His Heart was emptied unto the last Drop. "Take courage," He says, "I have overcome the world." I reply, "Lord, what wilt Thou have me do?"

APPEAL for PARDON

ACCEPT, O Lord, this appeal for pardon wrung from our afflicted and repentant souls, and in true sorrow for our sins and the sins of our relatives and friends.

We ask Pardon, O Divine Heart! for public scandals and evil living « for all who try to stir up disorder « for all who corrupt Thy little ones « for those who spend their youth and fortune in sensuous living « for crimes in families « the sins of parents and children.

We ask Pardon, O Divine Heart! for those who traffic in public crime « for those who lead and lure souls to eternal damnation by riches and corrupt literature « for those who excite evil passions by immodest fashions, corrupt plays and degenerate art.

We ask Pardon, O Divine Heart! for all attacks against our Holy Father the Pope « for all organized disobedience against Holy Mother the Church « for all weak and straying souls « for sinners who resist grace « for all abuse of the Sacraments or any outrage against the Holy Eucharist. Amen.

SEVEN OFFERINGS of the PRECIOUS BLOOD

« recited at the Monastery during the Night Prayers of the Sisters Adorers of the Precious Blood »

ETERNAL FATHER « I offer Thee the merits of the Most Precious Blood of Jesus, Thy Beloved Son and my Redeemer « for the propagation and exaltation of my dear Mother the Holy Church « for the safety and prosperity of her visible Head, the Holy Roman Pontiff « for the cardinals, bishops and pastors of souls « and for all the ministers of the sanctuary.

Glory be to the Father, etc. Blessed and praised forevermore be Jesus Who hath saved us by His Precious Blood!

ETERNAL FATHER « I offer Thee the merits of the Most Precious Blood of Jesus, Thy Beloved Son and my Divine Redeemer « for the peace and concord of nations « for the conversion of the enemies of our holy faith « and for the happiness of all Christian people.

Glory be to the Father, etc. Blessed and praised forevermore be Jesus Who hath saved us by His Precious Blood!

ETERNAL FATHER « I offer Thee the merits of the Most Precious Blood of Jesus, Thy Beloved Son and my Divine Redeemer « for the repentance of unbelievers « the extirpation of all heresies « and the conversion of sinners.

Glory be to the Father, etc. Blessed and praised forevermore be Jesus Who hath saved us by His Precious Blood!

ETERNAL FATHER « I offer Thee the merits of the Most Precious Blood of Jesus, Thy Beloved Son and my Divine Redeemer « for all my relations, friends and enemies « for the poor, the sick, and those in tribulation « and for all those for whom Thou willest I should pray, or knowest that I ought to pray.

Glory be to the Father, etc. Blessed and praised forevermore be Jesus Who hath saved us by His Precious Blood.

ETERNAL FATHER « I offer Thee the merits of the

Most Precious Blood of Jesus, Thy Beloved Son and my Divine Redeemer « for all those who shall this day pass to another life « that Thou mayest preserve them from the pains of Hell « and admit them the more readily to the possession of Thy Glory.

Glory be to the Father, etc. Blessed and praised forevermore be Jesus Who hath saved us by His Precious Blood.

ETERNAL FATHER « I offer Thee the merits of the Most Precious Blood of Jesus, Thy Beloved Son and my Divine Redeemer « for all those who are lovers of this Treasure of His Blood « and for all those who join with me in adoring and honoring It « and for all those who try to spread devotion to It. . . . *Glory be, etc.*

ETERNAL FATHER « I offer Thee the merits of the Most Precious Blood of Jesus, Thy Beloved Son and my Divine Redeemer « for all my wants, spiritual and temporal « for the holy souls in Purgatory « and particularly for those who in their lifetime were most devoted to this Price of our Redemption, and to the sorrows and pains of our dear Mother, most Holy Mary . . . *Glory be, etc.*

BLESSED and exalted be the Blood of Jesus, now and always, and through all eternity. Amen.

Last Will and Testament

Loose the nails now; take Him down,
He's stretched . . . and taut . . . and *dried!*
No felon this that hangs here dead,
No bleaching corpse with rigid head,
A parchment white, inscribed in red,
This Christ they crucified!

Take Him down, with reverent care,
He's fragile . . . costly . . . dear!
Parchment written on with whips,
Penned with sharpened leaden tips,
Paragraphed in livid strips,
Then stamped with iron spear!

Take Him down . . . How can I read
A message high above?
Ah! Now I see. This vellum thin
Appears a document wherein
Men have written . . . hate . . . and sin,
And God has written . . . Love!

Then fold Him gently; guard Him well,
Envault Him in a tomb.
A covenant in Death's disguise,
Here a five-sealed charter lies
That grants the joy of Paradise,
That ends eternal doom!

J. W. L. in Columbia

MEMORARE to our
LADY of the PRECIOUS BLOOD

REMEMBER, O Lady of the Precious Blood, the sorrowful Sheddings of the Blood of your Jesus and the most bitter tears you mingled with His Redeeming Blood.

In the name of the Blood of the Victim of Reparation and of thy holy tears « in the name of the seven swords which pierced thy heart, by which you became the Co-Redemptress of the human race and the Queen of Martyrs «have pity on my soul and on all its miseries » have pity on sinners and on the innocent souls they seek to pervert « have pity on the poor, the sick, the infirm, on all their sufferings, both physical and moral « have pity on the agonizing, especially upon those who, except for thine intercession, would leave this world without being purified in the Blood of the Lamb.

It is by the Blood of your Dying Son, by His inexpressible Sufferings, by His last plea to His Father in favor of mankind, by His ignominious Death and by the perpetuation of His Sacrifice on Catholic Altars « that I beg you not to reject my supplications, but graciously to hear them. **Amen.**

CONSECRATION to MARY

MOST HOLY MARY, my Lady, to thy faithful care and particular protection and to the bosom of thy mercy« today and every day, and particularly at the hour of my death« I consecrate my soul and my body« all my hope and consolation« all my trials and miseries« my life and the end of my life I commit to thee,

that through thy most holy intercession and by thy merits, all my actions may be directed and ordered according to thy will and that of thy Divine Son. Amen.

For CHILDREN before BIRTH

MARY, Immaculate Mother, I beseech thee by the joy that thou didst experience in the birth of Jesus, Thy Divine Son, to take under Thy motherly protection all the little ones that are to be born this day throughout the world.
Obtain for them the grace of holy Baptism. Watch over them always. Pray that from the day when they receive for the first time the God of love, their hearts, pure and innocent, may ever respond to the beatings of the Eucharistic Heart of Jesus, and attach themselves to Him forever. Amen.

MY ROSARY

 HE ROSARY of our Blessed Mother is a framework of meditations on the Precious Blood. There are fifteen Mysteries « of the Joys « Sorrows « Glories of her Jesus and ours.

The ROSARY is a pilgrimage on which Mary accompanies us to the Holy Places sanctified by Christ's Life, Death, Resurrection.

AS A DAILY PRAYER it is the prayer dearest to Our Lady. The oftener we say it, the more we shall love it. It brings us the special blessing of God, particularly when the family recites it together. On Indulgenced Beads, it is powerful in relieving souls in Purgatory.

AS A NOVENA PRAYER. At Naples in 1884 Our Blessed "Queen of the Rosary" appeared and promised: "Whoever desires to obtain favors from me, should make THREE Novenas in Petition and THREE Novenas in Thanksgiving." For 54 days in succession you recite the Rosary « a long Novena, but it is a Novena of Love « a test of your faith, perseverance, sincerity. No prayer is in vain or goes unheard.

TO JESUS THROUGH MARY. In each of the five Joyful, Sorrowful and Glorious

Mysteries, Mary shows us a picture of Christ. We shall meditate on it. We shall also ask for the grace each Mystery suggests.

JOYFUL MYSTERIES — Monday, Thursday

1. **ANNUNCIATION:** to be the messenger of God's Truth.

2. **VISITATION:** to obtain love for neighbor.

3. **BIRTH OF CHRIST:** to make room for Christ in the inn of your soul and body.

4. **PRESENTATION OF JESUS:** to obtain respect for God's Will.

5. **FINDING OF JESUS:** to obtain grace of searching for and finding Him.

SORROWFUL MYSTERIES — Tuesday, Friday

1. **AGONY OF JESUS:** to conform oneself to God's Will.

2. **SCOURGING:** to obtain spirit of purity.

3. **CROWNING WITH THORNS:** to obtain moral courage.

4. **CARRYING OF CROSS:** to obtain patience in adversity.

5. **CRUCIFIXION:** to obtain sorrow for sin.

GLORIOUS MYSTERIES
Sunday, Wednesday, Saturday

1. **RESURRECTION:** to obtain increase of a live faith in hearing and heeding divine Truth.

2. **ASCENSION:** to obtain increase of hope in God's grace now and glory hereafter.

3. **DESCENT OF HOLY SPIRIT:** to obtain increase of love.

4. **ASSUMPTION:** to obtain devotion to Mary.

5. **CROWNING OF MARY:** to obtain grace of perseverance.

The ANGELUS

MEDITATION—thinking it over! A salute! two minutes, especially at noontime! a salute to Mary, Mother of God! through whom came Jesus, true God, true Man. History attests that when Peter the Hermit ordered the recital of the Angelus every day, victory was never wanting to the crusaders' arms. Today, the tongue of the Angelus Bell is your tongue praising Mary.

RECITE the ANGELUS

"The Angel of the Lord declared unto Mary and she conceived by the Holy Spirit." (*Hail Mary.*)

"Behold the handmaid of the Lord « be it done to me according to thy word." (*Hail Mary.*)

"And the Word was made Flesh and dwelt among us." (*Hail Mary.*)

Pray for us, O Holy Mother of God « that we may be made worthy of the promises of Christ.

LET US PRAY. Pour forth, we beseech Thee, O Lord, Thy Grace into our hearts; that we to whom the Incarnation of Christ Thy Son was made known by the message of an Angel, may by His Passion and Cross be brought to the glory of His Resurrection. Through the same Christ our Lord. Amen.

To PREVENT ONE MORTAL SIN

*If every day we begged Mary for grace to hinder
ONE mortal sin, what a year's service to God
and souls!*

O MARY, Immaculate Mother of
Jesus, we beseech thee, offer to
the Eternal Father the Precious Blood
of Thy Divine Son, to prevent at least
one mortal sin from being committed
somewhere in the world today. Amen.

CONVERSION or RETURN to FAITH

O GOD, all hearts are in Thy Hands.
Thou canst bend, as it pleases
Thee, the most stubborn, and soften
the most obdurate. I beseech Thee by
the Holy Name, the Precious Blood,
the Merits, Wounds and Divine Heart
of Jesus, Thy Beloved Son, to grant the
conversion we ask. Amen.

EJACULATIONS

SACRED HEART OF JESUS, Thy Kingdom
come.

SWEET HEART OF JESUS, have mercy on
us and all our brethren who have gone
astray.

O MARY, most sorrowful mother of all
Christians, pray for us.

NECESSARY to SALVATION

(Composed by Pope Clement XI, 1721)

O MY GOD, I believe in Thee; do Thou strengthen my faith. All my hopes are in Thee; do Thou secure them. I love Thee; teach me to love Thee daily more and more. I am sorry that I have offended Thee; do Thou increase my sorrow.

I adore Thee as my first beginning; I aspire after Thee as my last end. I give Thee thanks as my constant benefactor; I call upon Thee as my sovereign protector.

Vouchsafe, O my God! to conduct me by Thy wisdom, to restrain me by Thy justice, to comfort me by Thy mercy, to defend me by Thy power.

To Thee I desire to consecrate all my thoughts, words, actions and sufferings; that henceforward I may think of Thee; speak of Thee, refer all my actions to Thy greater glory and suffer willingly whatever Thou shalt appoint.

Lord, I desire that in all things Thy will may be done because it is Thy will, and in the manner that Thou willest.

I beg of Thee to enlighten my understanding, to inflame my will, to purify my body and to sanctify my soul.

Give me strength, O my God! to expiate

HOME and FOREIGN MISSIONS

¶ *Why only 300,000,000 Catholics out of 1,500,000,000? Did Jesus die for me only? To preserve my faith, I must propagate it. Until I pray or give alms to the missions, I am not worthy of the name of Christian.*

O MERCIFUL JESUS, Savior of mankind, Who hast commissioned Thine Apostles and their successors to preach the Gospel to every creature « bless the work of the apostolic men and women who labor in the home and foreign missions to save souls redeemed by Thy Precious Blood.

To our LADY, HELP of CHRISTIANS

« for loyalty to Holy Mother Church »

MARY, Immaculate Virgin, Mother of God and our Mother « thou seest how the Catholic Faith is assailed by the devil and the world « that Faith in which we purpose by the help of God, to live and die. To thee we entrust our firm purpose of never joining assemblies of heretics. Do thou, all holy, offer to thy Divine Son our resolutions, and obtain from Him the graces necessary for us to keep them unto the end. Amen.

Mary, help of Christians, pray for us.

For SOCIAL JUSTICE

O MERCIFUL JESUS Who didst have compassion on the multitude, look down upon us in the depths of that spiritual depression, which is the root of all our temporal misery. Behold the widespread envy and discontent in private and public life because men seek not first Thy Kingdom and Justice. Give to us, we beseech Thee, and to our elected leaders the wisdom and strength to do Thy Holy Will in keeping respect for the dignity of labor by a decent living wage; in protecting family life from divorce and sins against nature; in upholding religious and political liberty; in restoring Thee to our schools of learning. To whom shall we go, if not to Thee, since only Thou, by the example of Thy Human Life and the strength of Thy Divine Grace can supply the ideals and incentive to realize these principles of social justice and social charity, fully aware, as we are, that unless Thou, the Lord, build the house, they labor in vain who build it. Amen.

PROTECTION AGAINST ACCIDENTS

When you start out each day or before each auto trip, make the Sign of the Cross and say: "MAY Jesus, Mary and Joseph be with us on our way. St. Christopher, pray for us."

PRAYER for our CITY

LOOK DOWN, Holy Father and Lord from Thy Sanctuary, and from Heaven, Thy dwelling-place on high « and behold this Sacred Victim, which our Great High Priest, Thy Holy Child, our Lord Jesus, offers up to Thee for the sins of His brethren « and be appeased for the multitude of our sins. Behold, the voice of the Blood of Jesus, our Brother, cries to Thee from the Cross. Give ear, O Lord. Be appeased, O Lord! Hearken and do not tarry, for Thine Own Sake, O my God, for Thy Name is invoked upon this city and upon Thy people « and deal with us according to Thy Mercy. That Thou vouchsafe to defend, pacify, keep, preserve, and bless this city, we beseech Thee to hear us.

In TIME of SICKNESS

O DIVINE PHYSICIAN, Thou Who hast always loved to console and heal the sick of body and mind, give me patience to bear this suffering in reparation for the sufferings which I and others have inflicted on Thy Crucified Body. By Thy Power, relieve the sharpness of my pain and exhaustion but above all, kind Jesus, heal the wounds of my soul. Even though I find it hard to pray, yet shall I ever say, "Thy Will be done." Amen.

For NURSES

 O WONDROUS Angel of the Agony, sent by the Father to strengthen and encourage His Son, as He lay prostrate in Gethsemane, obtain for me, I beseech Thee, the grace to understand more clearly my sublime vocation of a Christian Nurse, so that I may more intelligently, faithfully, and generously dedicate myself to my Savior, now suffering in the sick, Who with the Father and the Holy Ghost, liveth and reigneth, world without end. Amen.

TO JESUS, CROSS-CARRIER

O JESUS! by that Wound which Thou didst suffer on Thy Shoulder from carrying Thy Cross « have mercy, I entreat Thee, on those who have a lifelong cross to bear « and also upon those who have secret sorrows which only Thou canst know. May the memory of Thy painful Cross-bearings give them strength to carry theirs, with courage and loyalty to the end. May the thought of that secret Suffering Thou didst endure, teach them to sanctify their hidden sorrows that they may be fruitful for Thy Glory. Amen.

In TIME of MY AFFLICTION

BLESSED, O Lord, be Thy Name forever, Who hast permitted this affliction to come upon me. I cannot escape it, but must of necessity fly to Thee to help me and turn it to my good.

Lord, I am now in affliction. My soul is ill at ease, for I am much troubled with this present suffering. Let it please Thee, Lord, to deliver me, for, poor wretch that I am, what can I do without Thee? Thy mighty Hand can do all things.

Give me patience, O Lord, and strength and peace. Help me, my God, and I will not fear, no matter how grievously I may be afflicted. Lord, "Thy Will be done." Welcome be the Will of God.

"Sacred Heart of Jesus, I place my trust in Thee."

In TIME of CALAMITY

O LORD JESUS CHRIST, true God and true Man, God of Sanctity, God of Majesty, God Everlasting « have pity on us and on the whole human race. « Now and always purify us from our sins and infirmities with Thy Precious Blood « so that we may be able to live in Thy holy peace and charity, now and forever. Amen.

STUDENTS! *Pray . . .*

to Sanctify and Increase Study

Praying to Jesus as Teacher, to Mary as Mother of true education, assures success in daily study, at examination time and on the Commencement Day of Eternity. "When I look at Jesus and Mary," said St. Edmund, "my understanding receives more light and my bodily eyes are kept from tiring."

To JESUS « O merciful God, grant me the grace that I may eagerly desire all that is pleasing to Thee, examine it carefully, acknowledge it truthfully, and fulfill it perfectly to the praise and glory of Thy Name. Amen.

O Lord, preserve to us the Faith.

To MARY « O dearest Mother, by thine Immaculate Conception, I wish to place all my studies under thy direction, and I declare that I chiefly study in order to spread greater glory to God and devotion to thee. Therefore, I beseech thee, most loving Mother, Seat of Wisdom, to assist my work and I promise to give the proper thanks for any success I obtain, to thine intercession with God. Amen.

Our Lady of Good Studies, pray for us.

MY VOCATION IN LIFE

¶ *Pray fervently to make the right choice of your future life. On it depends the happiness of your own soul and other souls in this life and for all eternity.*

BEHOLD ME at thy feet, O Virgin most kind, seeking to obtain through thee the most important grace of knowing what I ought to do. « I desire nothing but to comply perfectly with the Will of thy Divine Son at every moment of my life. « Mother of Good Counsel, let me hear thy voice. It will dispel every doubt that troubles my mind.

I trust in thee, being confident that, since thou art the Mother of my Redeemer, thou wilt also be the Mother of my salvation. « If thou, O Mary, wilt not send me a ray of the Divine Sun, what light will enlighten me? Who will direct me if thou refusest, who art the Mother of the uncreated Wisdom?

Listen, then, to my humble prayers. Let me not be lost in my uncertainty and instability « lead me along the straight road that ends in life everlasting « thou, who art my only hope, and whose hands are full of the riches of virtue and of life, and who dispensest the fruits of honor and holiness.

INCREASE of VOCATIONS
to Priesthood and Religious State

¶ *The modern urge for riches, comfort and pleasure is preventing many young men and women from consecrating their lives to the service of Christ and the salvation of souls. To some who may be hesitating and in need of your prayers, Jesus says: "Why do you stand here all day idle? Go you also into the vineyard."*

O GOD, Who dost not desire the death of a sinner, but rather that he be converted and live « grant, we beseech Thee, through the intercession of Blessed Mary, ever Virgin, and of all the Saints « an increase of laborers for Thy Church « who, co-operating with Christ, may give themselves for the salvation of souls « through the same Jesus Christ, Thy Son, Our Lord, Who liveth and reigneth with Thee in the union of the Holy Spirit world without end. Amen.

MARY, Queen of the Clergy, obtain for us a great number of holy priests.

O LORD, bless Thy Church with holy Priests and fervent Religious.

My BODY

¶ *"Do you not know that your bodies are members of Christ? . . . (and) the temple of the Holy Spirit . . . You have been bought at a great price. Glorify God and bear Him in your body."* 1 Cor. 6: 15, 19, 20.

¶ *"I exhort you, brethren . . . to present your bodies as a sacrifice, living, holy, pleasing to God—your spiritual service."* Romans 12, 1.

O MY GOD, Thou Who hast given me a body to keep pure and clean and healthy for Thy service and my eternal happiness, forgive me for all my unfaithfulness in this great responsibility. Forgive me for every mean use which I have made of Thy gifts in thought, word or deed since my rebirth as Thine own adopted child in Baptism and my registration as a soldier of Jesus on the day of my Confirmation.

Create in me a clean heart, O God, and give me a steadfast will that I may be a strength to others around me. Teach me to reverence my body and the bodies of my fellow creatures. Help me to see the glory of perfect manhood in Jesus Christ and of perfect womanhood in Mary Immaculate. Inspire me with such love for the ideals for which our Savior lived and died, that all my passions and energies will be caught up into the enthusiasm of His service and evil things will lose their power. May my body be the servant of my soul, and may both body and soul be Thy servants, through Christ, our Lord. Amen.

For THOSE in SERVICE

O ETERNAL FATHER, I beseech Thee, watch over our beloved ones in the armed services of our Country. Do Thou recall how they were once reborn in the baptismal font as Thy children . . . and how later they were confirmed as soldiers of Thy Son, Jesus Christ. May they ever salute Him as their Commander-in-Chief and with Him march shoulder to Shoulder unto final Victory. Give them such a strong faith that no human fear may ever

cause them to betray their Baptismal
Vows and Confirmation Pledge. O
Mother Mary, thou who didst raise thy
Son to be our Soldier, show thyself a
Mother unto them now and at the hour
of their death. Amen.

NATIONAL ORDER and INTERNATIONAL PEACE

O KING OF PEACE, Thou Who didst
shed Thy Precious Blood that all
men might live as brothers in loving
harmony, we humbly prostrate ourselves before Thee to deplore our
many sins of revolt against Thee and
our neighbor. In Thy Mercy, O Lord,
we implore Thee to inspire each and
all of us to observe Thy Command-
ments and the teachings of Thy Gospel;
to inspire our rulers also to heed the
wise and fatherly counsels of our Holy
Father the Pope, Thy representative on
earth, so that peace may again be en-
joyed by men of good will and greater
glory be given to Thee. Amen.

PRAY for the DYING

¶ *Today 80,000 souls will die. Pray now for those dying. Tomorrow will be too late. This daily practice, so simple, so helpful should appeal to every Catholic. One soul saved each day means 365 each year. What a rich harvest of souls to present unto God! What a rich harvest of prayers they will offer for your soul when you, too, are in need!*

PRAYER for the DYING

O MOST MERCIFUL JESUS, Lover of souls « I pray Thee, by the agony of Thy most Sacred Heart, and by the sorrows of Thine Immaculate Mother « cleanse in Thine Own Blood the sinners of the whole world who are now in their agony and who are to die this day. Amen.

HEART OF JESUS, once in agony, have pity on the dying.

The Uncompleted Painting

To the **DYING JESUS**

MY CRUCIFIED JESUS, mercifully accept the prayer which I now make to Thee « for help in the moment of my death, when, at its approach, all my senses shall fail me.

¶ *Death prevented the completion of the above picture « a painting intended for our Sanctuary. The artist, Rudolph Schmalzl, had already finished the mural paintings on our Monastery walls. He was working on the above picture when death came.* HE DIED WITH HIS FACE TOWARDS CHRIST'S *« such a death to which we should all aspire and pray »*

IN THE MORNING

Hear your loved ones softly pleading
From the green graves lonesome lying
Ever crying:
"Have pity! you at least, my friends" ...

FOR and TO the SOULS

O ALL YOU ANGELS of Consolation, go and visit those patient sufferers, offer for them the merits of the Sacred Hearts of Jesus, Mary, and Joseph, and obtain their speedy union with Jesus, Whose vision is bliss, and Who yearns to have them with Him. O sweet brethren, so mightily afflicted! knowing your fear and love of God, and your charity for souls, pray for us that we may speedily obtain what we now ask for our urgent needs and also the grace of a good life and a holy death.

IN THE NOONTIME

While the hot skies far are glowing
Think of pain no relief knowing,
Their prison fires appalling
Their piteous voices calling:
"Have pity! you at least,
                    my friends" . . .

For OUR OWN

GOOD JESUS, Whose loving Heart was ever troubled by the sorrows of others, look with pity on the souls of our dear ones in Purgatory. O You Who "loved Your Own" hear our cry for mercy, and grant that those whom You called from our homes and hearts, may soon enjoy everlasting rest in the home of Thy Love in Heaven. Amen.

Eternal rest grant unto them, O, Lord.
And let perpetual light shine on them.
Amen.

IN THE EVENING

In the time of sad remembrance
Give a prayer to old friends gone
Let your heart with mournful greeting
Hear their sad appeal repeating:
"Have pity! you at least,

my friends" . . .

HEROIC ACT of LOVE

¶ *It does not prevent you from praying for yourself, for your friends or any other intention. By this* "HEROIC ACT OF LOVE" *you merely give up to the Holy Souls the satisfaction you make for the temporal punishment due to your sins.*

¶ *Should you go to Purgatory, God will apply to you the prayers for the souls in Purgatory which those on earth are ever offering up to Him. Those souls who may be released from their sufferings by your Heroic Act, will never prove ungrateful. In turn they will pray for you.*

IN THE NIGHTTIME

By the love in life you bore them
By the tears in death shed o'er them
By their words and looks in dying
Hear their plaintive voices crying:
"Have pity! you at least,

my friends" . . .

HEROIC ACT of LOVE

¶ *The Church calls this Act "HEROIC." Few acts of our lives deserve to be called HEROIC. We cannot afford to throw away this opportunity to make an "HEROIC ACT OF LOVE." Make it for the Love of God.*

DEAR LORD, for the Love of Thy Precious Blood, I wish to make an heroic offering of all the good works I do in life « in satisfaction for the temporal punishment due to my many sins « and of all the prayers offered up for me after death « in favor of those souls whom Our Blessed Mother wishes to deliver from the pains of Purgatory. Amen.

Prayer for EMPLOYMENT

O SON of God and Son of the Virgin Mary, Thy Sacred Heart is an ocean of mercy, compassion, and love for all men—but especially for the poor.

To Thee I come, filled with confidence, to place my prayer for work in Thy Sacred Heart.

Thou didst come to preach the gospel to the poor—Thou didst labor with Thine Own Hands—Thou didst consecrate poverty by choosing it for Thine Own Life.

O Sacred Heart of Jesus, hear my prayer for work, and in Thy Mother's name grant my request. Amen.

In his desire to see the cult of the most Precious Blood of Christ, the Immaculate Lamb, by Whom we were redeemed, grow from day to day, His Holiness, Our Pontiff, Pope John XXIII has deigned to approve the following Litany, composed and given by the Sacred Congregation of Rites. « Feb. 24, 1960 »

THE LITANY OF THE MOST PRECIOUS BLOOD

Lord, have mercy on us,
   Christ, have mercy on us.
Lord, have mercy on us.
Christ, hear us,
   Christ, graciously hear us.
God, the Father of heaven,
   Have mercy on us.
God, the Son, Redeemer of the world,
   Have mercy on us.
God, the Holy Spirit,
   Have mercy on us.
Holy Trinity, One God,
   Have mercy on us.

Blood of Christ, only-begotten Son of the Eternal Father, *Save us.*

Blood of Christ, Incarnate Word of God, *

Blood of Christ, of the New and Eternal Testament,

Blood of Christ, falling upon the earth in the Agony,

Blood of Christ, shed profusely in the Scourging,

Blood of Christ, flowing forth in the Crowning with Thorns,

Blood of Christ, poured out on the Cross,

Blood of Christ, price of our salvation,

Blood of Christ, without which there is no forgiveness,

Blood of Christ, Eucharistic drink and refreshment of souls,

Blood of Christ, stream of mercy,

Blood of Christ, victor over demons,

Blood of Christ, courage of martyrs,

Blood of Christ, strength of confessors,

Blood of Christ, bringing forth virgins,

* *Save us.*

Blood of Christ, help of those in peril,*

Blood of Christ, relief of the burdened,

Blood of Christ, solace in sorrow,

Blood of Christ, hope of the penitent,

Blood of Christ, consolation of the dying,

Blood of Christ, peace and tenderness of hearts,

Blood of Christ, pledge of Eternal Life,

Blood of Christ, freeing souls from Purgatory,

Blood of Christ, most worthy of all glory and honor,

* *Save us.*

Lamb of God, Who takes away the sins of the world, *Spare us, O Lord.*

Lamb of God, Who takes away the sins of the world, *Graciously hear us, O Lord.*

Lamb of God, Who takes away the sins of the world, *Have mercy on us.*

V. You have redeemed us, O Lord, in Your Blood.

R. And made us, for our God, a kingdom.

Let us pray

ALMIGHTY and Eternal God, You have appointed Your only-begotten Son the Redeemer of the world, and willed to be appeased by His Blood. Grant, we beg of You, that we may worthily adore this price of our salvation, and through its power be safeguarded from the evils of this present life, so that we may rejoice in its fruits forever in heaven. Through the same Christ our Lord. *Amen.*

Glory be to the Father, and to the Son, and to the Holy Ghost.

As it was in the beginning, is now, and ever shall be, world without end.

Amen.

𝒯HE psalms are prayers in which God Himself teaches us how to pray; for they were written under the direct inspiration of the Holy Spirit. Herein we have the answer to the question: "What prayers shall I say?" Why the prayers of Holy Scripture itself! "There is no need to scrape together endless man-made prayers when Sacred Scripture frames the very thoughts of God." The psalms are the vital presentation of God's inspirations and man's aspirations; they are the ideal manifestations of man's hunger and thirst after God and of God's loving response to man. Of great age, they are ever new and appropriate. They are as satisfying and stimulating to us of the twentieth century as they were to men before the birth of Christ and down through the Apostolic and Middle Ages.

How to Pray the Psalms

𝒲E must make these psalms the expression of our own personal prayer-life. In the enemies of which David speaks so frequently, we can see our own spiritual enemies, satan, sin and temptation. The deep love for Jerusalem expressed by the psalmist we can take over and apply to the Church, to Christ Himself.

NOTE: The Psalm Readings were taken from "My Daily Psalm Book" by Rev. Msgr. Joseph B. Frey.

A Plea for Mercy in Time of Distress

PSALM 6

O LORD, reprove me not in thy anger, * nor chastise me in thy wrath.

3. Have pity on me, O Lord, for I am weak; * heal me, O Lord, for my very bones are shaken,

4. And my soul is deeply troubled; * but thou, O Lord, how long . . . ?

5. Return, O Lord, and save my life, * rescue me for thy mercy's sake.

6. For in death no one remembers thee: * who praises thee in the abode of the dead?

7. I am worn out with my sighing, night after night I moisten my bed with weeping, * with tears I drench my couch.

8. My eye is dim because of grief, * has grown old because of all my enemies.

9. Depart from me, all you evildoers, * for the Lord has heard my tearful cry.

10. The Lord has heard my pleading, * the Lord has accepted my prayer.

11. Let all my foes be brought to shame and utter confusion; * let them turn back and speedily be brought to shame.

Penitential Prayer of a Sick Person

PSALM 37, i

REBUKE me not, O Lord, in thy anger, * nor chastise me in thy wrath.

3. For thy arrows have pierced me, * and thy hand has come down upon me.

4. There is no soundness in my flesh because of thy wrath, * there is no health in my bones because of my sin.

5. For my guilt has overwhelmed me, * like a heavy load it weighs me down.

6. My wounds are foul and festering * because of my folly.

7. I am bent, I am bowed down exceedingly, * all day long I go about mourning.

8. For my loins are filled with burning pains, * and there is nothing healthy in my flesh.

9. I am benumbed and badly crushed, * I cry aloud because of the wild surging of my heart.

10. All my desire is known to thee, O Lord, * and my sighing is not hidden from thee.

11. My heart throbs, my strength is leaving me, * and the very light of my eyes fails me.

12. My friends and my companions

stand aloof from my affliction, * and
my relatives stand afar off.

13. They who seek my life lay snares,
and they who seek to injure me threat-
en ruin, * and scheme treachery all
day long.

God Our Only Refuge

PSALM 37, ii

BUT I, like one deaf, hear not, *
and I am like a dumb man who
opens not his mouth.

15. And I am like a man who hears
not, * and like one in whose mouth
there is no retort.

16. For in thee, O Lord, I trust: * thou
wilt answer me, O Lord, my God.

17. For I say: "Let them not rejoice
over me; * when my foot slips, let them
not become arrogant towards me."

18. For I am ready to fall, * and my
grief is ever with me.

19. For I confess my guilt, * and I am
uneasy because of my sin.

20. But powerful are they who oppose
me without reason, * and numerous
are they who hate me unjustly;

21. And they who repay evil for good, *
are my foes, because I seek to do good.

22. Forsake me not, O Lord, * my God,
be not far from me!

23. Hasten to help me, * O Lord, my salvation!

A Penitential Prayer

PSALM 101, i

O LORD, answer my prayer, * and let my cry come to thee.

3. Hide not thy face from me * in the day of my distress.

Incline thy ear to me: * when I call thee, answer me speedily.

4. For my days vanish like smoke, * and my bones burn like fire.

5. My heart, scorched like grass, is withering away, * I forget to eat my food.

6. Because of the violence of my moaning, * my bones cleave to my skin.

7. I am like a pelican in the wilderness, * I have become like an owl among ruins.

8. I am sleepless and I moan * like a solitary bird on the housetop.

9. My enemies are always insulting me; * they who rage against me, swear by my name.

10. For I eat ashes like bread, * and mingle my drink with tears,

11. Because of thy indignation and thy

wrath, * for thou hast lifted me up and
cast me down.
12. My days are like lengthened shad-
ows, * and I am withering away like
grass.

God is Faithful to His Promises

PSALM 101, ii

BUT thou, O Lord, dost abide forever, * and thy name throughout
all ages.
14. Arise and have pity on Sion, * because now is the time for thee to be
gracious to it, for the hour has come.
15. For thy servants love its stones, *
and they have pity on its ruins.
16. Then the nations will fear thy
name, O Lord, * and all the kings of
the earth thy glory,
17. When the Lord restores Sion * and
appears in his glory.
18. When he regards the prayers of
the needy, * and does not reject their
prayer.
19. Let this be written for a future
generation, * and let a people yet un-
born praise the Lord.
20. For the Lord has looked down from
his sanctuary on high, * from heaven
he has looked upon the earth,

21. To hear the groans of the captives, * to set free those doomed to death,

22. That the name of the Lord might be proclaimed in Sion, * and his praise in Jerusalem,

23. When the peoples are gathered together * and the kingdoms, to serve the Lord.

PSALM 101, iii

HE has worn out my strength in the way, * he has shortened my days.

25. I say: O my God, take me not away in the midst of my days; * thy years endure throughout the ages.

26. Of old thou didst found the earth, * and heaven is the work of thy hands.

27. They shall perish, but thou wilt endure, * and all things shall grow old like a garment.

As raiment thou changest them, and
28. they are changed: * but thou art the same, and thy years have no end.

29. The children of thy servants shall dwell securely, * and their offspring shall endure before thee.

A Penitential Prayer

PSALM 129

O UT of the depths I cry to thee, O
Lord, * O Lord, hear my voice!
2. Let thy ears be attentive * to the
voice of my supplication.
3. If thou shouldst remember sins, O
Lord, * O Lord, who could bear it?
4. But with thee is forgiveness, * that
thou mayest be served with reverence.
5. I hope in the Lord, * my soul hopes
in his word;
6. My soul waits for the Lord, * more
than watchmen for the dawn.
More than watchmen for the dawn, *
7. let Israel wait for the Lord,
For with the Lord is mercy * and with
him plenteous redemption:
8. And he shall redeem Israel * from
all its sins.

A Penitential Prayer

PSALM 142

O LORD, hear my prayer, listen to
my entreaty according to thy
faithfulness, * answer me according
to thy justice.
2. Bring not thy servant to trial, * for
in thy sight no man living is just.

3. For the enemy pursues me: he has crushed my life to the earth, * he has made me to dwell in darkness like those long dead.

4. And my spirit faints within me; * my heart within me grows numb.

5. I recall the days of old, I meditate on all thy deeds, * I consider the works of thy hands.

6. I stretch out my hands to thee; * my soul thirsts for thee like parched land.

7. Hasten to answer me, O Lord: * for my spirit fails.

Hide not thy face from me, * lest I become like those who go down into the pit.

8. Let me experience thy mercy speedily, * for I trust in thee.

Show me the way in which I should walk, * for to thee I lift up my soul.

9. Deliver me from my enemies, O Lord: * in thee I hope.

10. Teach me to do thy will, * for thou art my God.

Thy spirit is good: * may it guide me on level ground.

11. For thy name's sake, O Lord, save my life; * in thy mercy bring me out of distress.

12. And in thy kindness cut off my

enemies, and bring to naught all who afflict me: * for I am thy servant.

Homesickness for God's House

PSALM 41, i

AS the deer longs for the streams of water, * so does my soul long for thee, O God.

3. My soul thirsts for God, for the living God: * when shall I come and see the face of God?

4. My tears have become my food day and night, * while they say to me daily: "Where is thy God?"

5. I keep thinking of this and I pour out my very spirit: how I used to walk with the crowd, * and lead them to the house of God, amid the sounds of joy and praise, * in a festive gathering.

6. Why art thou dejected, O my soul, * and disturbed within me?

Hope in God; for I shall again praise him, * my savior and my God.

Hope in God

PSALM 41, ii

MY soul is depressed within me: * so I will think of thee from the land of the Jordan and Hermon, from the hill of Misar.

8. Deep calls unto deep with the roar of thy waterfalls: * all thy breakers and thy waves have passed over me.

9. By day may the Lord send his mercy, * and at night I will sing to him, I will praise the God of my life.

10. I say to God: my Rock, why hast thou forgotten me? * why must I go about sorrowful, afflicted by my enemy?

11. My bones are being crushed, while my foes taunt me, * while they say to me daily: "Where is thy God?"

12. Why art thou dejected, O my soul, * and disturbed within me?

Hope in God: for I shall again praise him, * my savior, my God.

Prayer for Confidence

PSALM 10

IN the Lord I take refuge; how can you say to me: * "Fly away like a bird to the mountain!

2. For, see the wicked bend the bow, they fit their arrow to the string, * to shoot in the dark at the upright of heart.

3. When the foundations are overthrown, * what can the just man do?"

4. The Lord is in his holy temple; * the Lord's throne is in heaven.

His eyes see, * his glances test the
children of men.

5. The Lord tries the just and the
wicked; * he hates the lover of evil.

6. He will pour down burning coals
and brimstone upon the wicked; * the
scorching wind shall be the portion of
their cup.

7. For the Lord is just, he loves justice; * the upright shall behold his face.

Praise the Lord, Our Only Refuge

PSALM 33, i

I WILL bless the Lord at all times: *
his praise shall be ever in my
mouth.

3. Let my soul glory in the Lord: * let
the humble hear and rejoice.

4. Glorify the Lord with me; * and let
us together exalt his name.

5. I sought the Lord, and he answered
me; * and he delivered me from all my
fears.

6. Look unto him, that you may be
filled with joy, * and your face be not
covered with shame.

7. Behold, the poor man cried, and the
Lord heard, * and helped him out of all
his troubles.

8. The angel of the Lord encamps

round those who fear him, * and he
rescues them.

9. Taste and see how good the Lord
is; * happy the man who takes refuge
in him.

10. Fear the Lord, you his faithful
ones, * for nothing is wanting to those
who fear him.

11. The powerful have become poor
and hungry; * but they who seek the
Lord shall not lack any good thing.

Blessings of the Faithful Soul

PSALM 33, ii

COME, children, listen to me; * I
will teach you the fear of the Lord.

13. Who is the man who loves life, *
desires length of days to enjoy prosperity?

14. Keep thy tongue from evil, * and
thy lips from deceitful words.

15. Depart from evil and do good; *
seek peace and pursue it.

16. The eyes of the Lord are upon the
just, * his ears open to their cry.

17. The face of the Lord is against
evil-doers, * to destroy the remembrance of them from the earth.

18. The just cried and the Lord an-

swered them; * and delivered them from all their troubles.

19. The Lord is close to the brokenhearted, * and saves those of contrite spirit.

20. Many are the trials of the just man; * but the Lord delivers him from all.

21. He guards all his bones: * not one of them shall be broken.

22. Evil shall slay the wicked, * and they who hate the just shall be punished.

23. The Lord delivers the souls of his servants, * and whoever flees to him for refuge shall not be punished.

Prayer in Time of Temptation

PSALM 55

HAVE mercy on me, O God, for men do trample upon me. * They oppress and attack me without ceasing.

3. My foes are forever treading on me, * for many fight against me.

4. O Most High, in the day when fear comes upon me, * I will trust in thee.

5. In God, whose promise I praise, in God I put my trust, I will not fear: * what can man do to me?

6. All day long they disparage me, *

all their thoughts are against me, unto harm.

7. They gather together, they lie in wait, they watch my footsteps, * seeking my life.

8. Repay them for the evil, * in wrath, O God, cast down the peoples.

9. Thou hast kept account of the ways of my exile; my tears are kept in thy water-skin: * are they not recorded in thy book?

10. Then shall my enemies turn back, whenever I call upon thee; * by this I know well that God is on my side.

11. In God, whose promise I praise,

12. in God I put my trust, I will not fear: * what can man do to me?

13. I am held to the vows, O God, which I made to thee, * I will fulfill the thank-offerings to thee,

14. For thou hast delivered my life from death, and my feet from stumbling, * so that I may walk before God in the light of the living.

Prayer of Confidence

PSALM 26, i

THE Lord is my light and my salvation: whom shall I fear? * The Lord is the defense of my life:

whom shall I dread?

2. When evildoers assail me, to devour me, * my enemies and my foes, they stumble and fall.

3. Though an army should encamp against me, my heart shall not fear; * though war should rise against me, even then will I trust.

4. One thing I ask of the Lord, this do I seek: * that I may dwell in the house of the Lord all the days of my life,
To enjoy the graciousness of the Lord, * and to behold his temple.

5. For he will hide me in his tent in the day of adversity, * he will shelter me in the secret place of his tabernacle, he will set me high upon a rock.

6. Even now my head is lifted up * above my enemies round about me,
And I will offer joyful sacrifices in his tabernacle, * I will sing and chant praises to the Lord.

PSALM 26, ii

NEAR, O Lord, my voice which cries to thee, * be gracious to me and answer me.

8. My heart speaks to thee, my face seeks thee; * thy face, O Lord, I seek.

9. Hide not thy face from me, * rebuff not thy servant in anger.

Thou art my help; cast me not off, *
nor forsake me, O God, my savior.

10. Though my father and my mother
abandon me, * yet will the Lord receive me.

11. Teach me thy way, O Lord, * and
lead me along a safe path because of
my enemies.

12. Deliver me not to the desires of
my foes, * for false witnesses have
risen up against me, and men who
breathe violence.

13. I believe that I shall behold the
goodness of the Lord * in the land of
the living.

14. Wait for the Lord, be strong, *
and let thy heart take courage, and
wait for the Lord.

An Act of Contrition

PSALM 50

HAVE mercy on me, O God, according to thy mercy; * according
to thy great clemency blot out my iniquity.

4. Wash me completely from my guilt, *
and cleanse me from my sin.

5. For I acknowledge my iniquity, *
and my sin is always before me.

6. Against thee only have I sinned, *

and I have done what is evil in thy sight,

This I confess that thou mayest be known to be just in thy sentence, * right in thy judgment.

7. Behold, I was born in guilt, * and my mother conceived me in sin.

8. Behold, thou dost delight in sincerity of heart, * and teachest me wisdom in the depths of my soul.

9. Sprinkle me with hyssop, that I may be cleansed; * wash me, that I may become whiter than snow.

10. Let me hear sounds of joy and gladness, * let the bones which thou hast crushed rejoice.

11. Turn away thy face from my sins, * and blot out all my guilt.

12. Create a clean heart for me, O God, * and renew in me a steadfast spirit.

13. Cast me not off from thy presence, * and take not thy holy spirit from me.

14. Restore to me the joy of thy salvation, * and strengthen me with a generous spirit.

15. I will teach the unjust thy ways, * and sinners shall be converted to thee.

16. Deliver me from blood-guilt, O God, God my savior: * let my tongue rejoice because of thy justice.

17. O Lord, open thou my lips, * and my mouth shall declare thy praise.

18. For thou dost not delight in sacrifice; * and a burnt-offering thou wouldst not accept, if I offered it.

19. My sacrifice, O God, is a contrite spirit, * a contrite and humbled heart, O God, thou wilt not despise.

20. In thy goodness, O Lord, deal kindly with Sion, * that thou mayest rebuild the walls of Jerusalem.

Then wilt thou accept lawful sacrifices, oblations and burnt-offerings, * then will they offer bullocks on thy altar.

Act of Thanksgiving After Confession

PSALM 31

HAPPY is he whose iniquity is forgiven, * whose sin is pardoned.

2. Happy the man to whom the Lord imputes no guilt, * and in whose spirit there is no deceit.

3. As long as I was silent, my bones wasted away * amid my continual groanings.

4. For day and night thy hand lay

heavy upon me, * my strength was sapped as with summer heat.

5. My sin I confessed to thee, * and my guilt I did not hide;
I said: I confess my iniquity to the Lord, * and thou didst forgive the guilt of my sin.

6. Therefore every pious man will pray to thee * in time of need.
When the floods rush in, * they will not reach him.

7. Thou art a refuge to me, thou wilt guard me against distress, * with the joy of my salvation thou wilt surround me.

8. I will instruct thee, and direct thee in the way thou shouldst walk; * I will counsel thee, and keep my eyes fixed upon thee.

9. Be not like the horse and the mule, without understanding, whose temper is curbed by bit and bridle, * else they will not approach thee.

10. Many are the sorrows of the wicked; * but kindness surrounds him who hopes in the Lord.

11. Be glad in the Lord, and rejoice, you just; * and be jubilant, all you upright of heart.

The Two Ways
PSALM 1

HAPPY the man who follows not *
the counsel of the wicked,
Nor enters upon the path of sinners, *
nor sits in the assembly of the insolent;
2. But his delight is in the law of the
Lord, * and he meditates on his law
day and night.
3. And he is like a tree * planted be-
side streams of water,
That yields fruit in due season, whose
leaves do not wither, * and whatever
he does, prospers.
4. Not so the wicked, not so, * but they
are like chaff which the wind scatters.
5. Therefore the wicked shall not stand
firm in the judgment, * nor sinners in
the gathering of the just.
6. For the Lord takes care of the way
of the just, * but the course of the
wicked shall end in ruin.

The Messianic King
PSALM 2

WHY do the nations rage, * and
the peoples plot in vain?
2. The kings of the earth rise up and
rulers conspire together * against the
Lord and His anointed:

3. "Let us break their bonds * and cast their fetters from us!"

4. He who dwells in heaven laughs, * the Lord mocks them.

5. Then in his anger he speaks to them,* and in his wrath he dismays them.

6. "I, indeed, have set up my king * on Sion, my holy hill!"

7. I will proclaim the decree of the Lord: The Lord said to me: * "Thou art my son, this day have I begotten thee.

8. Ask of me and I will give thee the nations for thy inheritance, * the ends of the earth for thy possession.

9. Thou shalt rule them with an iron rod; * thou shalt shatter them like a potter's vessel."

10. Now then, O kings, be wise; * take warning, O judges of the earth.

11. Serve the Lord in fear, and rejoice in him; * with trembling offer homage to him,
Lest he be angry, and you perish, when suddenly his anger is enkindled: * happy are all who take refuge in him.

Prayer of Thanksgiving
PSALM 17, i

I LOVE thee, O Lord, my strength, *
3. O Lord, my rock, my fortress,
my deliverer.

My God, my rock of refuge, * my
shield, the strength of my salvation,
my stronghold!

4. I will call upon the Lord, most
praiseworthy, * and I will be safe from
my foes.

5. The waves of destruction engulfed
me, * and the torrents of iniquity terri-
fied me;

6. The bonds of hell surrounded me, *
the snares of death enmeshed me.

7. In my distress I called upon the
Lord, * and unto my God I cried out;
And from his temple he heard my
voice, * and my cry came to his ears.

8. The earth shook and trembled, the
foundations of the mountains quaked *
and rocked, because he was burning
with rage.

9. Smoke rose from his nostrils, and
from his mouth a devouring fire, *
fire-brands were enkindled by him.

10. He lowered the heavens and came
down, * and a dark cloud was under
his feet.

11. He rode upon a Cherub and he flew, * and he soared on the wings of the wind.

12. He put on darkness as a veil, * dark waters and dense clouds as his covering.

13. Because of the brightness of his face * burning coals were kindled.

14. And the Lord thundered from heaven, * and the Most High gave forth his voice.

15. And he sent forth his arrows and scattered them, * much lightning, and routed them.

16. Then the depths of the sea appeared * and the foundations of the world were laid bare
At the rebuke of the Lord, * at the blast of the breath of his wrath.

Prayer of Thanksgiving
PSALM 17, ii

HE reached forth from on high, he grasped me, * he drew me out of many waters.

18. He rescued me from my mighty foe, * and from my enemies, who were too strong for me.

19. They attacked me in the day of my misfortune, * but the Lord was my support,

20. And he led me forth into an open space, * he saved me, because he loves me.

21. The Lord dealt with me according to my righteousness, * according to the cleanness of my hands has he rewarded me,

22. For I have kept the ways of the Lord, * and have not departed from my God by sinning,

23. For I have kept all his ordinances before my eyes, * and his statutes I did not set aside.

24. But I stood before him without stain, * and kept myself from all fault.

25. So the Lord rewarded me according to my righteousness, * according to the cleanness of my hands in his sight.

26. With the kind thou showest thyself kind, * with the perfect thou dost act perfectly,

27. With the pure thou showest thyself pure, * but with the perverse thou dealest craftily.

28. For thou dost save an humble people, * but haughty eyes thou bringest low.

29. For thou dost light my lamp, O

Lord; * my God, thou dost enlighten
my darkness.
30. For through thee I can charge
against armed forces, * and with the
help of my God I can scale a fortress
wall.
31. God's way is perfect, the word of
the Lord is fire-tried; * he is a shield
for all who take refuge in him.

Prayer of Thanksgiving

PSALM 17, iii

FOR who is God but the Lord? *
or who is a rock but our God.
33. The God who girded me with
strength * and made my way perfect,
34. Who made my feet as fleet as the
feet of stags, * and set me firmly upon
high ground,
35. Who trained my hands for battle, *
and my arms to bend the brazen bow.
36. And thou gavest me thy saving
shield, thy right hand upheld me, *
and thy care made me great.
37. Thou hast widened the way for my
steps, * and my feet have not faltered.
38. I pursued my enemies and over-
took them, * nor did I turn back, until
I had slain them.

39. I smote them and they could not rise, * they fell beneath my feet.

40. For thou didst gird me with strength for battle, * and bend my adversaries beneath me.

41. For thou hast put my enemies to flight, * and scattered those who hated me.

42. They cried out — and there was none to save them; * unto the Lord— and he heard them not.

43. And I scattered them as dust before the wind, * I stamped them down as the dirt of the streets.

44. Thou hast delivered me from the strife of the people, * thou hast made me the head of the nations.

45. A people I knew not, became my servants, * they obeyed me, as soon as they heard of me.

46. Foreigners flattered me, foreigners grew pale, * they came out trembling from their fortresses.

47. The Lord lives, and blessed be my Rock, * my God, my savior, be exalted,

48. The God who has avenged me * and made peoples subject to me.

49. Thou who hast freed me from my foes, and raised me above my adver-

saries, * thou hast saved me from the man of violence.

50. Therefore will I praise thee among the nations, O Lord, * and chant a hymn to thy name:

51. Thou who hast granted great victories to the king and shown kindness to thy anointed, * to David and his descendants forever.

The Good Shepherd

PSALM 22

THE Lord is my shepherd: I want for nothing; * he makes me rest in green pastures.

He leads me to waters where I may rest; * 3. he revives my spirit.

He guides me along the right paths * for his name's sake.

4. Even though I walk in a dark valley, * I will fear no evil, for thou art with me. Thy rod and thy staff: * these comfort me.

5. Thou settest a table for me * in the sight of my enemies;

Thou anointest my head with oil; * my cup overflows.

6. Goodness and kindness shall follow me * all the days of my life,

And I shall dwell in the house of the Lord * for a long time.

Acts of Confidence
PSALM 30, i

TO thee, O Lord, I flee for refuge: let me never be put to shame; * in thy justice deliver me!

3. Incline thy ear to me, * make haste to rescue me.

Be to me a rock of refuge, * a fortress to save me.

4. For thou art my rock and my stronghold, * and for thy name's sake thou wilt lead me and guide me.

5. Thou wilt bring me out of the net which they have hidden for me, * for thou art my refuge.

6. Into thy hands I commend my spirit: * thou wilt redeem me, O Lord, faithful God.

7. Thou hatest the worshippers of empty idols; * but I trust in the Lord.

8. I will be glad and rejoice because of thy kindness, for thou hast seen my misery, * and in my distress thou hast helped me.

9. Thou hast not delivered me into the power of the enemy, * but thou hast set my feet in a spacious place.

Confident Prayer in Distress

PSALM 30, ii

HAVE pity on me, O Lord, for I am in trouble; * my eye grows weak with grief, my soul and my body.

11. For my life is spent in sorrow, * my years in groaning.

My strength has failed through affliction, * and my bones have wasted away.

12. I have become an object of scorn to all my enemies, a mockery to my neighbors, and an object of terror to my friends, * they who see me in public, flee from me.

13. I am fully forgotten, as one dead, * I am like a broken vessel.

14. For I have heard the whispering of the crowd—terror is everywhere! * plotting against me, they plan to take my life.

Prayer Answered: Deep Gratitude

PSALM 30, iii

NOW great is thy goodness, O Lord, * which thou hast reserved for those who fear thee,

Which thou showest to them who have

recourse to thee, * in the sight of men.

21. Thou shieldest them with thy presence * from the conspiracies of men.
Thou hidest them in thy tent * from the wrangling of tongues.

22. Blessed be the Lord, for he has shown me * his marvelous mercy in a fortified city.

23. Yet I said in my anxiety: * "I am cut off from thy sight:"
But thou hast heard the voice of my pleading, * when I cried to thee.

24. Love the Lord, all his devoted servants! * the Lord guards the faithful,
But he repays fully * those who act haughtily.

25. Take courage and let your heart be strengthened, * all who hope in the Lord.

Confidence in God

PSALM 45

GOD is our refuge and our strength; * he has indeed proved himself a great help in times of distress.

3. Therefore we do not fear, though the earth be overthrown, * and the mountains crash into the midst of the sea.

4. Let its waters roar and rage, * let the mountains be shaken by its violence:
The Lord of hosts is with us; * the God of Jacob is our stronghold.

5. The streams of the river gladden the city of God, * the holy dwelling place of the Most High.

6. God is in the midst of it, nor shall it be disturbed; * God will help it at the break of day.

7. Nations were in tumult, kingdoms tottered; * his voice thundered, the earth dissolved:

8. The Lord of hosts is with us; * the God of Jacob is our stronghold.

9. Come, behold the works of the Lord, * what wonders he has done upon earth.

10. Who makes wars to cease even unto the ends of the earth, * he breaks the bows and shatters the spears, and the shields he burns with fire.

11. Desist and know that I am God, * exalted among the nations, exalted on earth.

12. The Lord of hosts is with us; * the God of Jacob is our stronghold.